MOTIVATING
THE TEENAGE MIND

Eva Hoffman

with Martin Hoffman

Speechmark

First published in 2012 by

Speechmark Publishing Ltd, Sunningdale House, 43 Caldecotte Lake Drive, Milton Keynes MK7 8LF, United Kingdom

Tel: +44 (0)1908 277177   Fax: +44 (0)1908 278297

www.speechmark.net

002-5795 Printed in the United Kingdom by CMP (UK) Limited

British Library Cataloguing in Publication Data
A catalogue record for this book is available from the British Library

ISBN 978 0 86388 918 9

FSC
www.fsc.org
MIX
Paper from
responsible sources
FSC® C004309

Contents

Dear Teacher

Attempting to awaken motivation in older children and teenagers is probably the most demanding part of your work. No doubt you are already doing a lot that works for you and your students. Yet, the fact that you are reading this book suggests that, like many teachers we have worked with, you are still searching for new ways to arouse in your students an interest in learning.

Over 90 per cent of teachers we have spoken to admitted that it is reward, withdrawal of reward or punishment that dominate their everyday attempts to get students to do their work. While these methods result in some level of success with some students and in some circumstances, they do not solve the problem of motivation in many others.

Every force meets with resistance. Forcing students to do something they don't want to do generates resentment, anger and withdrawal of goodwill.

Working through the activities in this programme you may be reminded of techniques you haven't used for a while or have forgotten about; we hope you will also discover something new, something that will work for you and your students.

Before you start

Do every activity yourself before giving it to students

Your own experience in matters of personal development is at least as important as your knowledge. You may find that some activities challenge you, your life experiences, your mindset. As uneasy as it is for all of us, remind yourself that only when we find ourselves at the edge of our comfort zone, can we truly grow and develop.

Create an atmosphere of trust

When you use an activity, remember to suspend all judgment and accept every answer as valid. Encourage students to think about issues but don't insist that they share their thoughts with others. Establish the rule of absolute confidentiality and share your own experiences when appropriate. Your goal is to get them to think for themselves.

Brace yourself

When working with challenging teenagers, be prepared for all kinds of disruption. Giggles, sarcastic comments and generally 'playing up' often serve the purpose of covering insecurities, embarrassment, pain or anger. Laugh with your students, take deep breaths, move on to a different activity; anything to prevent emotional shutters from coming down.

At all times remind yourself to notice, respect and encourage your students

Make sure they know that you care about them, value them and that you believe in them *no matter what*!

We have constructed the programme around seven interrelated topics:

1 making and giving choices
2 awakening curiosity and interest
3 nurturing dreams and setting goals
4 making learning relevant
5 raising confidence
6 strengthening resilience
7 rewarding achievement

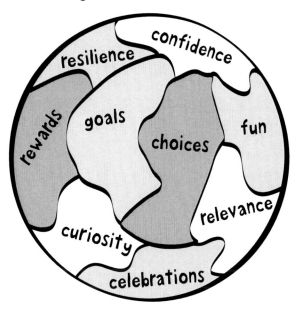

Choices

– are empowering
– provide a degree of freedom
– give a degree of control

Having no choice results in

– natural resistance to imposed tasks / ways of thinking
– anger or indifference

so motivation is poor or non-existent

Curiosity

– means wanting to know
– indicates readiness to find out / learn
– guarantees an open mind

Lack of curiosity and interest results in

– indifference
– dullness
– disengagement of senses

so motivation is poor or non-existent

Dreams and goals

– give awareness of purpose
– map the steps on the way
– provide inspiration

Lack of goals results in

– aimless drifting
– leaving everything to chance
– no vision for the future

so motivation is poor or non-existent

Relevance

– indicates a link between learning and self
– makes things meaningful
– provides a clear reason for learning

Seeing no relevance results in

– a negative attitude or indifference to the task
– a need to rebel
– learning only to pass exams

so motivation is poor or non-existent

Confidence

– makes resilience possible
– gives a positive outlook
– creates positive energy

Lack of confidence results in

– a sense of inadequacy
– deepening negativity (can't do it anyway)
– covering-up strategies (poor behaviour, aggression, withdrawal)

so motivation is poor or non-existent

Resilience

– makes experiencing success possible
– makes achieving goals possible
– boosts confidence

Lack of resilience results in

– inability to complete a project
– minimal chance of success
– poor sense of self-worth

so motivation is poor or non-existent

Rewards

– support resilience
– ease making steps towards goals
– boost confidence

Inappropriate rewards

– make people dependent on them
– seriously try resilience
– may result in poor self-motivation

Within each topic you will find:

- 'food for thought' for teachers
- activities to be introduced to students
- suggestions for how to do these activities
- inspirational quotations
- inspirational stories
- pictures / collages / graphs

What to invite students to do with...

Pictures / posters / collages / graphs

- interpret the meaning or possible meanings
- tell a story (real life or fantasy) based on the picture
- express the meaning in a picture / poster of your own (same idea – different image)
- make posters, collages, pictures illustrating an idea

Cards

- match: questions with answers, similar / opposing ideas
- sort different kinds of thoughts / ideas / information
- rearrange priorities
- pick a random card and share thoughts with a partner
- with quotes: interpret meaning – think of an example – own experience – same meaning in a different quote

Stories

- make a story board
- retell the story to someone who doesn't know it
- illustrate the story with posters / pictures / collages of your own
- find a different meaning / a moral
- pick key words you remember from the story

Expressing feelings and thoughts

- draw or paint a poster, a picture, a doodle
- talk – share with a partner or in small groups
- brainstorm, individually or in groups
- write a poem or rap
- tell someone / write what you are *not* feeling
- dance expressing your emotions and capture it on film
- act out using words or miming
- text someone you know

Pen and paper

- complete sentences
- fill in the blanks
- mark 'true' or 'false'
- circle / tick your answer
- sort into categories
- jot down your thoughts
- make a mind map

The programme may be delivered in a number of ways. However, we suggest you plan to do at least one activity every week.

Feel free to choose any activities suitable for your students from each of the seven parts of the programme. They are interrelated and interdependent. The programme will not have the desired effect on students if you focus on selected parts and omit others.

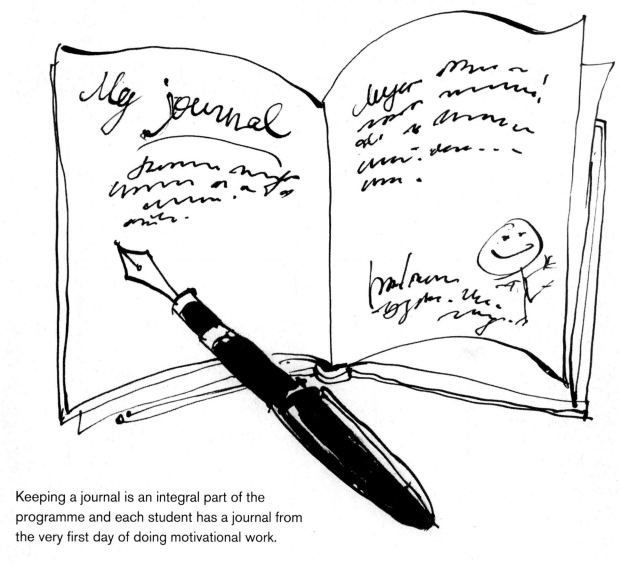

Keeping a journal is an integral part of the programme and each student has a journal from the very first day of doing motivational work.

The journal becomes a record of their journey towards self-motivation. It is a private document nobody can access but the student who owns it.

Unless students want to take their journals home, all journals need to be kept in a locked drawer to ensure privacy and confidentiality.

Rewarding achievement

Inappropriate rewards can be as harmful to students' self-esteem as inappropriate criticism.

Descriptive praise vs evaluative praise

Praise students using description rather than evaluation and be as specific as you possibly can.

Rather than saying 'excellent', 'good work', 'well done', 'good boy', say something like 'Your description paints a colourful and lively picture of the scene' and leave the evaluation to the student.

Descriptive praise is more helpful because it:

- is specific

- is meaningful

- shows that you have given the work due attention

- says exactly what has been done well

whereas evaluative praise:

- is general

- is often meaningless

- is dismissive

- doesn't teach anything because it doesn't specify what is good or how to make it better.

Practise giving descriptive praise and write your own examples below.

To reward or not to reward
Food for thought

In his book *The Motivated Mind* (2006), Raj Persaud quotes a number of psychologists who have expressed serious reservations about the long-term effectiveness of rewarding.

They say:

- Rewards often divert attention from the task to the reward product.

- People often play the system: they try to obtain maximum rewards for minimum effort.

- It was repeatedly found that rewarding people stopped them from continuing to do a task when no reward was available.

- Parents and teachers seem prone to being lured to a 'reward treadmill'.

- Many educators acknowledge the adverse effect of over-praising on learners.

- Grades seem to take away the satisfaction of learning something and result in students' 'grades-grabbing behaviour'.

- For many students learning is all about grades – the only thing most students are concerned with, and reinforced by the system.

- Rewards and punishment are often counterproductive because they undermine 'intrinsic motivation'.

- Teachers do little to awaken intrinsic motivation in students; instead they rely heavily on 'sticks and carrots'.

- Children and young people are not even aware that learning just to learn something and enjoying the process and the results is an option.

Which of the statements sound right to you?
Which do you strongly disagree with?

Which form of reward works best?

- Ask students to think about the last time they were rewarded.

- Ask them why exactly they did the work:

  – in order to be rewarded?

  – to avoid punishment?

  – for any other reason?

- Ask them when they were last punished and whether the punishment was effective.

  – Have they since done the same thing again?

- Once students have marked the effectiveness of the rewards listed overleaf, encourage them to choose three rewards which motivate them best to do their work / study.

- If you find out that the listed rewards fail to motivate students, ask what else could motivate them.

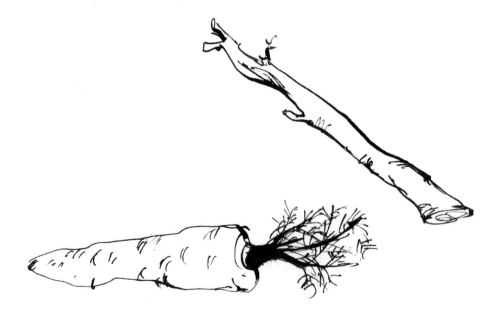

Which form of reward works best?

On a scale of 1–10 mark the effectiveness of each of these rewards.
10 = very effective, 1 = not effective.

1 2 3 4 5 6 7 8 9 10   A good grade

1 2 3 4 5 6 7 8 9 10   Praise from your teacher

1 2 3 4 5 6 7 8 9 10   Happiness of your family members

1 2 3 4 5 6 7 8 9 10   A present

1 2 3 4 5 6 7 8 9 10   A trip / holiday / party

1 2 3 4 5 6 7 8 9 10   A sticker / an award

1 2 3 4 5 6 7 8 9 10   Your satisfaction that you have succeeded

1 2 3 4 5 6 7 8 9 10   ....

1 2 3 4 5 6 7 8 9 10   ....

1 2 3 4 5 6 7 8 9 10   ....

Would you still work to achieve a goal if you were not going to be rewarded?

Teacher's page

You – the winner

It is a well-known fact that an important part of any sports champion's training is visualising every step of the performance and then seeing themselves as a winner.

When faced with a challenge, most of us make the mistake of imagining how things can go wrong rather than visualising a positive outcome.

The power of positive thinking cannot be overestimated. To give yourself a better chance to succeed in whatever you set out to do, you need to train yourself in the art of visualising a positive rather than a negative outcome to your efforts.

Encourage your students to do the same.

• Photocopy the sheet and tell students:

Glue in a standing photo of yourself. Draw:

– a laurel crown on your head

– a medal around your neck

– a winner's cup in your hand

– a pedestal under your feet

Feel the way you're going to feel.
See people congratulating you and smiling.
Hear what they will be saying.

Stay with the sensation for a while.

You – the winner

Glue a standing photo of yourself here.

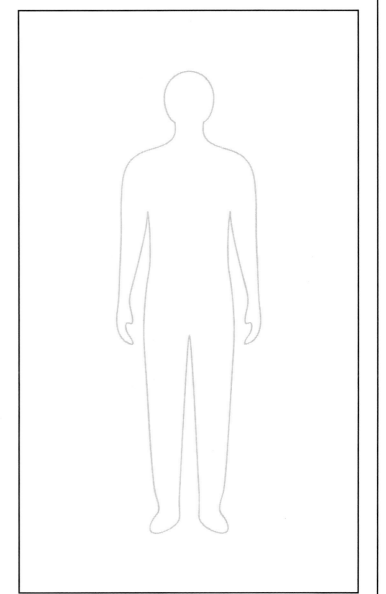

Draw:

– a laurel crown on your head

– a medal around your neck

– a winner's cup in your hand

– a pedestal under your feet

– crowds cheering.

Feel the way you're going to feel.
See people smiling and congratulating you.
Hear what they will be saying.

Stay with the sensation for a while.

The power of appreciation (1)

We all know how wonderful we feel when someone appreciates us. And yet many of us don't express our appreciation of others often enough.

To make appreciation truly meaningful, we need to make it as specific as possible.

Saying things such as: 'I appreciate your help' is nice, but how much more meaningful it would be to write a note that said:

'When you offered to help with my planning the other day, I was touched because I realised you really cared. Thank you so much.'

- Explore the meaning of appreciation:

  – recognition, acknowledgement, positive evaluation, applause, praise, an expression of good feelings about something, indication that what you are doing is helpful to others.

- Encourage everybody to think what it is they can be thankful for:

  – their health, peace in the country, food and water, someone who cares about them, being able to see, shelter, music, friends, family.

- Make an 'appreciation board' and let every student write on a sticky label one thing they appreciate in their life.

- Photocopy the worksheet and tell students to write a note of appreciation to a friend.

- Ask them:

  'Would you consider sending this letter? Would you like to receive such a letter? Would you rather tell the person that you appreciate what they have done?'

- Encourage students to write an appreciation note to themselves.

The power of appreciation (1)

Think of a person who has done something for you:

– given you good advice

– helped you out in a crisis

– supported your efforts

– showed you they cared.

– ....

– ....

Write a note to this person, saying exactly:

– what they have done

– how they have done it

– how it made you feel and expressing your gratitude.

Dear

Dear Me

Now write a letter to yourself, appreciating the things you do and the person you are. For the purpose of writing this letter focus only on your strengths and successes, leaving any weaknesses for another occasion.

213

The power of appreciation (2)

Most of us like, in fact expect, our efforts to be rewarded, even when doing things we are supposed to do. We enjoy being praised, hearing words of appreciation, receiving thank-you notes and thank-you gifts.

As we all know, giving can often be even more rewarding than receiving. It's good to learn to notice other people's efforts and achievements and to get into a habit of giving praise, expressing appreciation and congratulations, and sending thank-you notes.

- Ask students to make a list of people who have done something for them in the last few months.

- Tell them to write short thank-you notes to two people they have put on the list, stating specifically what they are thanking them for.

- Ask them to make another list of people they know who have succeeded in doing something well, no matter how big or small this something may be.

- Tell them to write two congratulatory notes to those whose achievement needs acknowledgment.

- If possible, give each student a couple of envelopes and encourage them to send or hand their notes to the people they have written to.

- Encourage student to develop a habit of thanking others for what they do and expressing appreciation for their efforts and achievements.

The power of appreciation (2)

Remember to say ...

On the notes attached to the board write who you could thank or congratulate and what you would be thanking or congratulating them for.

Four kinds of reward

Rewards may be divided into four categories, as shown in the pyramid below.

1 Avoidance
I do my work to avoid punishment.

2 Material
I do my work to get money.

3 Non-material
I do my work to be praised.

4 Personal growth
I do my work to feel satisfaction.

All the categories are potentially valid. However, the purpose of this activity is to draw students' attention to the all-important sense of own achievement, the glow we feel inside when we realise we have succeeded.

- Give students a copy of the worksheet and ask them to think about situations when they have been rewarded in these four ways.

- Ask students to write their thoughts in their journals.

- Encourage a discussion about rewards.

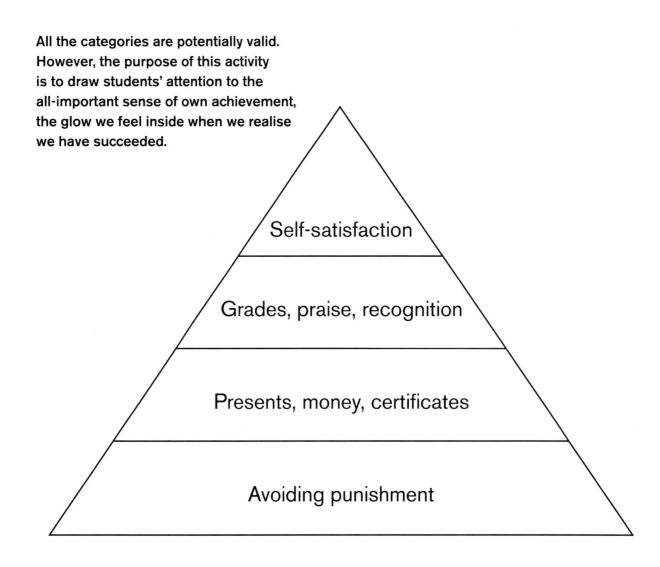

Four kinds of reward

Personal growth

Basic

fulfilment

SATISFACTION

feel-good

factor

AVOIDANCE

punishment

consequences

ReWaRdS

medals

PRAISE

appreciation

grades

MATERIAL

money

things

presents

Non-material

Material

What do you mostly do to avoid punishment?

What do you do to get something such as a good grade, an award, presents, money?

What do you mostly do in order to be praised and appreciated?

Do you do anything to have a sense of satisfaction that you've done something?

Give yourself some praise

We all know that praise has a motivating effect on students so we give it to them at every opportunity.

Some students shy away from praise. This may happen because they feel they haven't really achieved anything worth praising or because they don't like the 'fuss'.

Most students enjoy being praised but those who get a lot of it frequently get 'addicted' to hearing words of appreciation. When for some reason their good work goes unnoticed, they get upset, angry or even depressed.

To avoid getting upset when our achievements go unnoticed, we need to learn to give appreciation to ourselves.

- Tell students that it is possible that sometimes, for whatever reason, their good work may not receive due appreciation. This is why it makes a great deal of sense to learn to give appreciation to themselves.

- Ask students to write in the spaces provided on the worksheet four things they succeeded at. Tell them that it doesn't matter whether the successes are very small or big.

- Ask students to write next to teachers' comments what they will say to themselves when they succeed.

  – Well done, me!

  – Congratulations to me!

  – I am proud of myself. I have done well!

  – I am thrilled with my success!

Give yourself some praise

My achievement	Words I heard my teacher / parent say	Words I will say to myself

Reward yourself

Learning to reward ourselves is a crucial step to self-motivation.

Encourage students to develop their own system of self-rewarding.

Remind them that they are learning for themselves, not anybody else, and that no motivation is as important and powerful as self-motivation.

- Encourage a discussion about the value of rewarding oneself vs being rewarded by someone else.

- Ask students how they could reward themselves. If they are not forthcoming with ideas, here are some prompts:

  – go out with friends

  – watch a favourite video

  – have something nice to eat

  – go to a concert / cinema / theatre

  – get a present for yourself (a CD, a new top, a game)

  – sleep until lunchtime.

- If students say that they do all those things anyway, suggest that they come up with something special that will always be connected with a reward they can give to themselves.

- Talk with students about 'achievement'. Explain that this is not just about winning a competition or getting an Oscar or a Nobel Prize. Give examples of what achievement could be.

Reward yourself

How could you reward yourself for doing a good job?

Draw, doodle, scribble, glue in photos, paper cuttings, anything that will show how you could reward YOURSELF.

Reward yourself and celebrate your achievement every step of the way.

Inner glow

Think about the time when you were not expecting any material rewards, not even the appreciation of any specific person – the time when you were:

- **working and achieving results mainly to feel the satisfaction that comes with a job well done**

- **learning mainly in order to know and understand more**

- **helping others for no other reason but to feel that you have done something worthwhile.**

Remember what it felt like …

You may have experienced a sense of deep satisfaction, an almost physical sensation of warmth in your heart, an inner glow which brightened up your day and added a spring to your step. This may or may not happen very often but when it does, it feels good, really good. This very feeling is the reward for your efforts.

- Ask students to think whether they have ever done something they didn't have to do, knowing that the only reward would be their own satisfaction.

- If you see this is too much of a challenge, give them examples:
  - looking for some interesting facts on the internet
  - giving 20p to a small child buying some chewing gum because he is short of change
  - anonymously planting flowers in a public garden for everyone to enjoy.

- Ask students where in their bodies they feel the warmth and how they experience the inner glow:
  - around the heart
  - in the solar plexus (above the navel)
  - in the chest.

- Ask students how this 'inner glow' feels:
  - an 'expanding' chest
  - warmth around the heart
  - lightness
  - a smile within.

- Ask them to draw on the worksheet some kind of representation of the 'inner glow':
  - an orange ball
  - a whirl of colours
  - a big smiling heart

  and then glue it in their journal.

Inner glow

Remember when you have done something worthwhile, something you *didn't have to do*. Draw a picture which will best represent the feelings you experienced.

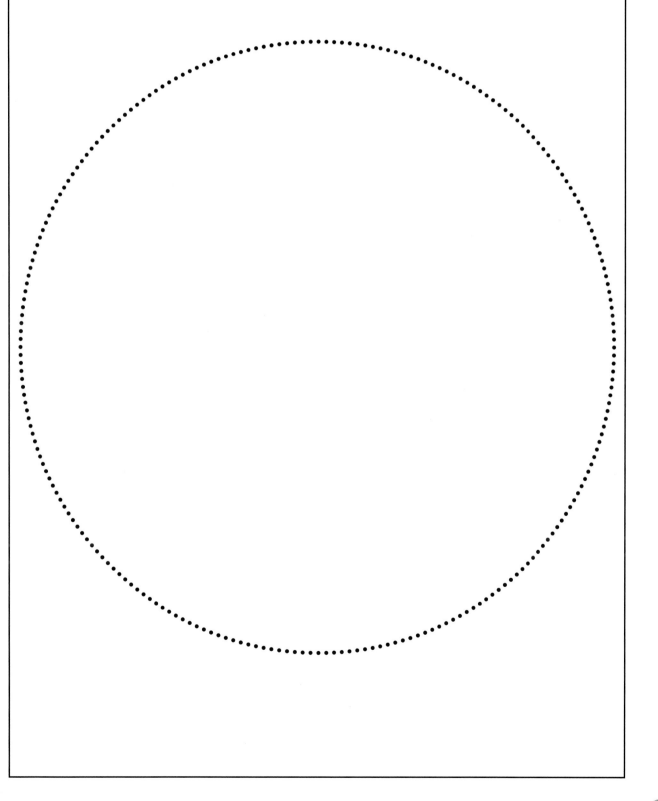

Do it for you

When students succeed in whatever they undertake to achieve, they often hear their parents or teachers say:

– 'I am so proud of you.'

– 'You have made your parents proud.'

– 'Your teacher will be delighted.'

On the one hand it is good to give praise; it obviously encourages people to do more of the required behaviour, raises their confidence and generally makes them feel better about themselves.

However, there is a danger that young people get the impression that they learn for somebody else rather than for themselves. They may think that they do the work because:

– this will please the teachers

– the school will do well in league tables

– parents / grandparents will be proud of them.

This way we are certainly not awakening students' intrinsic motivation, which is absolutely critical for self-esteem, confidence and long-term achievement.

Here is what you could do to give praise and at the same time awaken students' intrinsic motivation:

When a young person tells you that they have won a competition, got a very good grade, improved in spelling or received an award, rather than saying 'I am so proud of you', say 'This is wonderful! Are *you* proud of yourself? *You* can be really proud of yourself! I am delighted for you!'

- Ask students to write in the spaces provided on the worksheet two things they succeeded at. Tell them that it doesn't matter whether the successes are very small or big.

- Ask them to try to remember what their teacher or parent said to them and to write the comments below, eg:

  'Well done! I am proud of you! I knew you could do it!'

  or

  'At last you got your act together! You could've done better!'

- Tell students that no matter what people say, *they need to learn to appreciate their own achievement* and reward themselves with the feeling of satisfaction rather than wait for others to give them appreciation.

- Ask students to write below the teachers' comments what they will say to themselves when they succeed and encourage them to say the words aloud.

  Suggest:
  'I am proud of myself. I have done well! I am thrilled with my success!'

Do it for you

I am proud of myself

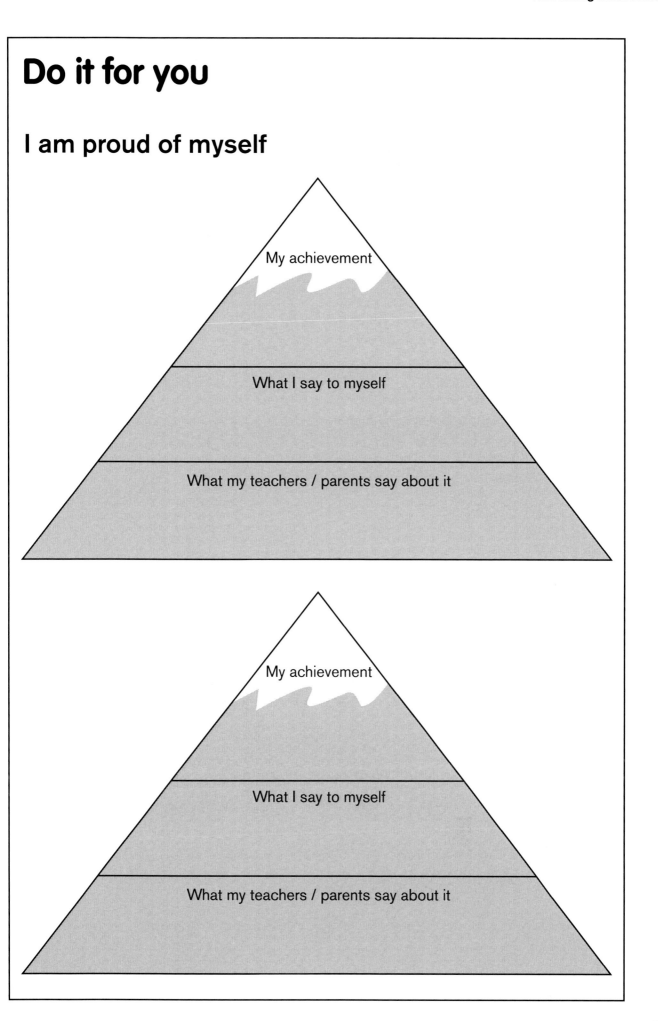

The meaning of your life

Every single day every one of us performs numerous and varied tasks. In our busy lives and all the ups and downs of daily existence it is easy to forget to stop and think about the purpose, the ultimate goal that lies beyond all those mundane tasks.

The story is about being able to see beyond the mundane daily tasks, to have a broader vision of the 'higher purpose' of whatever we do. The very awareness of our 'higher purpose', the meaning of our lives, can be the source of inspiration and a reward for our efforts. The 'cathedral' symbolises the 'higher purpose', the spiritual, (not necessarily religious!) aspect of life.

- Read the story to your students.

- Ask them what they think the meaning of the story is and, if necessary, give them your explanation.

- Talk about life purpose and give examples:

  – inspiring people and touching their lives

  – making discoveries (medical, technological etc.)

  – bringing up children – members of the next generation

  – enhancing communication between individuals, groups, nations

  – helping others live fulfilled lives

  – making people laugh / happy

  – giving people joy

  – making something people need

  – giving love and care

  – providing a necessary service

  – making life easier for others.

Every life has a purpose. It is sometimes hidden from our consciousness but it certainly is there! When we find it and embrace it, we begin to live a truly meaningful life.

The meaning of your life

The search

There was a Young Man who lived and worked in a big city. Most people he knew lived their lives earning money and spending it, earning and spending, earning and spending …

'What is the sense of all this?' thought the Young Man. 'Is that all there is to life?'

One day he decided to leave his job and travel around the world. He hoped that somewhere someone would help him find answers to the questions which kept burning in his brain.

The Young Man travelled for almost a year. He visited many countries, talked to many people, young and old, rich and poor, some well-educated, some not, some happy, some miserable. But not one person seemed able to help him find the answer he was seeking.

Then one day he came to a beautiful place in the mountains. At the top of a hill covered in flowering shrubs there was a huge building site. Everywhere he looked there were piles of stones, bricks, cement sacks and mountains of sand. As he approached the site, he spotted three men in dungarees sorting out bricks.

'Good morning!' said the Young Man. 'Lovely spot! Can you tell me what you are doing here?'

'Laying bricks, as you can see!' answered the tallest builder as he continued stacking bricks into his wheelbarrow.

'Earning my living, Governor,' said the second man, wiping sweat off his brow, 'and hard work it is, too!'

'I can surely see that,' said the Young Man and looked at the third man who had so far remained silent. The third man looked at the traveller, then into the sky, and said,

'As for me, Sir, I am building a cathedral'.

'Thank you, thank you so much!' exclaimed the Young Man and walked away with a spring in his step. Finally he had found his answer.

Questionnaires to assess the effectiveness of the programme

Motivating the Teenage Mind

This questionnaire needs to be completed by the student's teacher before starting the programme. Please circle your responses.

Student's name .... **Student's age** .... **Date** ....

In my opinion this student's

1 Attitude to school work is

very poor   poor   adequate   very good

2 Confidence in the ability to perform tasks is

very low   low   adequate   high

3 Behaviour in class is

unacceptable   bad   adequate   good

4 Overall grades are

very low   low   Cs   Bs and As

5 Handling of setbacks and challenging situations is

very poor   poor   adequate   good

Motivating the Teenage Mind

This questionnaire needs to be completed by the student's teacher once the student has gone through the programme. Please circle your responses.

Student's name .... Student's age .... Date ....

In my opinion this student's

1 Attitude to school work has

remained unchanged   improved a little   greatly improved

2 Confidence seems to have

remained unchanged   increased a little   increased a lot

3 Behaviour in class has

remained unchanged   improved a little   greatly improved

4 Grades

have remained unchanged   are a little better   are much better

5 Way of handling setbacks and challenging situations

has remained unchanged   has improved a little   is much better

231

Motivating the Teenage Mind

Student's end of programme questionnaire

1 Browse through your journal and give your general impression of every activity by grading them A, B, C, D or E, where A is most favourable.

2 Find the three most enjoyable activities

(a) ....

(b) ....

(c) ....

3 Find the three most useful activities

(a) ....

(b) ....

(c) ....

4 Find activities which seemed like a waste of time

5 What has changed as a result of the programme?

(a) The way I feel about my ability to learn

(b) The way I think about school

(c) ....

References

Bandura A (1977) *Social Learning Theory*, General Learning Press, New York.

Bird J (2006) *How to Change Your Life in 7 Steps*, Vermilion, London.

Branden N (1997) 'What self-esteem is and is not', adapted from Branden N (1997) *The Art of Living Consciously*, Simon & Schuster, New York.

Byrne R (2008) *The Secret: Daily Teachings*, Atria Books, New York.

Canfield J (2001) 'Preparing youth for the 21st century', keynote address at conference, San Francisco.

De Bono E (2007) *Do Bono's Thinking Course*, BBC Active, Harlow.

Gardner H (1985) *Frames of Mind*, Paladin, London.

Hoffman E (2001) *Introducing Children to their Intelligences*, Learn to Learn, Middlewich, Cheshire.

Hoffman E (2002) *Introducing Children to their Amazing Brains*, Learn to Learn, Middlewich, Cheshire.

Mayne B (2006) *Goal Mapping: How to Turn Your Dreams into Realities. The Practical Workbook*, Watkins, London.

Niebuhr R (1943) *The Serenity Prayer*.

Persaud R (2006) *The Motivated Mind*, Bantam, London.

Revell J & Norman S (2000) *In Your Hands: NLP in ELT*, Saffire Press, London.

Recommended reading

For teens

Bird J (2006) *How to Change Your Life in 7 Steps*, Vermilion, London.

Canfield J & Hansen MV (1993) *Chicken Soup for the Soul: Stories that Restore Your Faith in Human Nature*, Random House, London.

Canfield J, Hansen MV & Kirberger K (1997) *Chicken Soup for the Teenage Soul: 101 Stories of Life, Love, and Learning*, Health Communications, Deerfield Beach, FL.

Canfield J, Hansen MV & Kirberger K (1998) *Chicken Soup for the Teenage Soul II: 101 More Stories of Life, Love, and Learning*, Health Communications, Deerfield Beach, FL.

Covey S (1998) *The 7 Habits of Highly Effective Teens*, Simon & Schuster, New York.

Covey S (2004) *The 7 Habits of Highly Effective Teenagers, Personal Workbook*, Simon & Schuster, New York.

Hodgson D (2006) *The Buzz: A Practical Confidence Builder for Teenagers*, Crown House, Carmarthen, Wales.

Pelzer D (2007) *Help Yourself for Teens: Real-life Advice for Real-life Challenges Facing Teenagers*, Penguin Books, London.

Spencer J (2003) *Who Moved My Cheese? for Teens: An A-mazing Way to Change and Win!*, Vermilion, London.

For adults working with teens

Burnett G (2003) *Learning to Learn*, Crown House, Bancyfelin, Wales.

Feinstein S (2009) *Secrets of the Teenage Brain*, Corwin Press, Thousand Oaks, CA.

Gilbert I (2002) *Essential Motivation in the Classroom*, Routledge/Falmer, London & New York.

Gilbert I (2004) *The Big Book of Independent Thinking*, Crown House, Carmarthen, Wales.

Hemery D (2005) *How to Help Children Find the Champion Within Themselves*, BBC Worldwide, London.

Persaud R (2006) *The Motivated Mind*, Bantam, London.

Recommended motivational films

The Secret (Prime Time Productions, 2006)

Dead Poets Society (Touchstone Pictures, 1989)

Patch Adams (Universal Pictures, 1998)

What Dreams May Come (PolyGram Filmed Entertainment, 1998)

Forrest Gump (Paramount Pictures, 1994)

Field of Dreams (Universal Pictures, 1989)

City of Angels (Warner Bros, 1998)

It's a Wonderful Life (Paramount Pictures, originally RKO, 1946)

Cool Runnings (Walt Disney, 1993)

Lean on Me (Warner Bros, 1982)

Fried Green Tomatoes (Universal Pictures, 1991)

Ben Hur (MGM, 1959)

The Other Sister (Touchstone Pictures, 1999)

To Sir with Love (Columbia Pictures, 1967)

Stand by Me (Columbia Pictures, 1986)

The Colour Purple (Warner Bros, 1985)

Billy Elliot (Universal Focus, 2000)

Tuesdays with Morrie (Carlton America / Harpo Productions, 1999)

Amelie (UGC/Miramax, 2001)

Miracle (Walt Disney, 2004)

School of Rock (Paramount Pictures, 2003)

Mr Holland's Opus (Hollywood Pictures, 1996)

Dangerous Minds (Hollywood Pictures, 1995)

The Miracle Worker (United Artists, 1962)

Music of the Heart (Miramax, 1999)

The Karate Kid (Columbia Pictures, 2010)

Stand and Deliver (Warner Bros, 1988)

Sister Act (Touchstone Pictures, 1992)

Sister Act 2 (Touchstone Pictures, 1993)

Search for more inspirational films on the internet.

Making and
giving choices

*The life that you lead is to a large extent the result
of all the choices you have made up till now.*

Choices

Every day we make a number of small, often seemingly insignificant choices.

From time to time we make choices that may affect our lives. It is interesting to see how many choices we make; often many more than we think!

When students are young they may feel that they only do what they have to do and so they tend to rebel against the imposed will of others. It is empowering for students and young people to realise how many choices they can, in fact, make.

- Ask students to write every little thing they choose during the day, even if those little things feel totally unimportant.

- To get them started, give a few examples:
  - to have cereal or toast for breakfast
  - to wear a black top or a blue one
  - to play football with friends or watch a TV programme
  - to tell the truth about something or tell a few fibs
  - to do or not to do what Mum asked you to do.

- Tell students that there are no right or wrong answers here; whatever they come up with will be absolutely fine.

- Some students may choose to work with friends (another choice!).

- When the list is ready, ask students to:
  - mark with a '+' all choices which they think were good for them
  - mark with a '−' all choices which they would rather not make again.

Choices

Write a few things you chose to do (or not to do) yesterday. Then write some more. Write down every little choice you made that comes to mind. If necessary, write overleaf.

1 ....

2 ....

3 ....

4 ....

5 ....

6 ....

7 ....

8 ....

Rose-tinted spectacles or dark shades
Choosing the way you look at things

The purpose of the activity is to see that it is possible to go from one way of looking at things to another.

Two people looking at the same thing may see something very different. Some may see rain as an obstacle and a nuisance while others may take it as a saving grace. We may see a person as stubborn, but we may also describe them as determined. 'Stubborn' is not so good but 'determined' is a compliment.

If we wish, we may change the way we see some things.

What we see depends mainly on what we look for.

If we look for something good or pleasant, we are more likely to find it than when we focus on the bad and negative.

- Hand out the worksheet and ask students what they think the picture means.

- Ask them to put on their imaginary rose-tinted spectacles and find something good in one of the following:

  – a rainy day

  – short days in winter

  – not having much money

  – coming from a large family

  – being an only child.

- Now ask students to look at the same things wearing dark shades and see only the bad things about the above situations.

- Encourage students to consider whether it is always good to look at the world through rose-tinted spectacles or dark shades.

Rose-tinted spectacles or dark shades
Choosing the way you look at things

Half full or half empty?

The purpose of the activity is to help students see that it is possible to go from one way of looking at things to another *and that it depends on what they choose to focus on.*

Some people live with a constant feeling there is never enough: not enough fun, not enough food, not enough money, not enough time, not enough friends, etc. Others feel most of the time that there is plenty to go around.

The interesting thing is that how people feel does not depend on how much they have. There are some extremely rich people who are never satisfied with what they have and there are people who have little but somehow manage to enjoy what they have.

- Ask students what they think the way people feel about scarcity and abundance depends on.

- Either look at the glass on the worksheet or get a glass and half fill it with water.

- Ask students what they see: a half empty glass or a half full one?

- Encourage students to practise seeing the opposite to what they originally have seen; if their initial response has been half full, ask them to see the half that is empty, and the other way round.

Half full or half empty?

Is your glass half full or half empty?

Write in your journal what you have learnt about the way you look at things.

Your choices

If we are asked to reflect on our beliefs or the way we act and told that whatever we come up with is 'right', we tend to experience mixed emotions. We may feel inhibited, unsure, overwhelmed and sense that our mind goes 'blank'; or we may feel liberated and have ideas easily flowing out of our mind.

Practice in switching off our critical mind while allowing ideas to flow freely is a very useful activity. It allows us to be relaxed, open and playful. It is also very valuable for generating new ideas as we allow ourselves to see new connections and new possibilities. Once we have a few ideas on paper, we can switch on our critical mind and evaluate the results of the flow.

- Make students feel comfortable by letting them know that whatever they come up with is right. You will need to say it a number of times as students used to 'right or wrong' responses will find it difficult to believe you!

- Give a few examples of some trivial choices we make every day:

  – what to eat

  – what to wear

  – which film to watch.

- Talk with students about some important choices we make, the consequences of which may affect our whole life.

- Ask students to write on the worksheet a few important choices they have made in the past.

- Ask them to look at the choices and think which of them proved to be good and which ones they will not choose to make again.

- Do not insist students share their thoughts with you or anyone else; the purpose of the activity is for students themselves to come to some important realisations. They may want to keep these private.

Your choices

Write a few choices (big or small) you made yesterday:

1 ....

2 ....

3 ....

4 ....

5 ....

6 ....

7 ....

Now write a few important (for you) choices you have made this year:

1 ....

2 ....

3 ....

4 ....

5 ....

6 ....

7 ....

So what?
Choices and their consequences

Every choice we make has its consequences.

There is always a reason we choose to act in a certain way.

Do some of our choices:

– seem necessary for us to feel we fit in with our peers?

– help us avoid doing things we are scared of?

– result from a desire to be like someone else, someone we admire?

– make us feel strong and powerful?

- Photocopy the sheets for each student.

- Give out the first sheet. Tell students to focus on one potential choice and think of all possible outcomes.

- Give out the second sheet and ask students to find more consequences of the choice they selected.

- If appropriate do the same with other potential choices.

- Tell students that each choice has its short-term and long-term consequences. Very often we go for the short-term outcomes, choosing to ignore the long-term ones.

  - You choose to eat cakes, sweets, ice-cream and other snacks – the immediate result is pleasure; you don't want to think about all the fat and sugar going to your tummy and hips.

  - You choose to go out with your mates every day of the week – the result is the fun you have; you ignore that fact that you're getting behind with your work while the time for exams is getting dangerously close …

- Encourage students either to select possible consequences of their potential choices or to think of one short-term and one long-term consequence for each choice.

- Be prepared for jokes, sarcasm and silliness. These are only natural so don't let your students' reaction get to you. The message will still get through.

So what?
Choices and their consequences

Every choice we make has consequences, some good,
some bad and some neither good nor bad.

Match the CHOICES with their possible CONSEQUENCES.
One choice may have a number of different consequences.

If I choose…

to spend all my time having fun,

If I choose…

to focus my attention on the
good things in life,

If I choose…

to remember that there are people who
care about me,

If I choose…

to be a victim and feel angry with the
world,

If I choose…

to smoke / drink alcohol,

If I choose…

to set goals for my future,

…I might have no stress	**…I might** get ill and let somebody else worry about my problems
…I might start enjoying the good things in my life	**…I might** start treating my family better
…I might enjoy every minute	**…I might** feel I need to do something for others
…I might be grumpy, rude, unpleasant, possibly violent	**…I might** feel I fit in with my peer group
…I might live in 'cloud cuckoo land' and not have to face the realities of life	**…I might** sound silly and naïve to many people
…I might be seen as a boffin	**…I might** do something I will be proud of

So what?
Choices and their consequences

Self-reflection can be embarrassing and painful as it often touches our sensitive spots. Bear in mind that your students' giggles, sarcastic comments, rude jokes and other silliness serve as protection against embarrassment as well as a shield against pain.

Eeny, meeny, miny, mo

Every single day of our life, while going about our business, we make a great number of choices. Often we are not even aware we are actually making choices; we just do what we believe has to be done.

Becoming aware of the fact that we are, indeed, making choices can boost our confidence and the sense of control over our lives.

How do most of us make our choices?

– 'eeny, meeny, miny, mo'?

– heads or tails?

– 'the lesser of two evils'?

– a list of pros and cons?

– a gut feeling?

– ……………………………..?

Let's take credit for the good choices we make but avoid identifying with our choices, particularly if they prove to be the wrong ones. The fact that we've made some 'bad' choices doesn't make us bad people.

- Make a copy of the worksheet for each student.

- Remind students that this is primarily an awareness-raising activity and not an attempt to change what they do.

- Ask students to select one or two choices they may want to avoid in future.

- Encourage them to write their thoughts in their journal.

Eeny, meeny, miny, mo

Which ones do you usually choose?

Which ones would you like to choose more often?

Gossiping about a friend behind her back	or	loyally defending your friend against gossip
Going out with mates, leaving work not done	or	doing the work first
Being moody and grumpy	or	making an effort to restrain your bad mood (and smile?)
Leaving your bedroom looking like a tip	or	clearing the mess and tidying up the place
Pretending you don't see when someone is hurting a weaker person	or	defending the weaker person or trying to stop the fight
Failing to keep a promise you have made	or	keeping the promise although you don't feel like it
Lying about something to avoid unpleasant consequences	or	admitting your guilt despite fear of consequences
Swearing at someone because they have done it to you	or	zipping up your mouth, taking a deep breath and speaking later
Tearing something to pieces in anger	or	leaving the situation for a while to come back to it later

To have a choice or not to have a choice

Having no choice, not being able to make decisions about what we do and how we do things, frequently results in feelings of powerlessness, anger and frustration, or passivity and indifference.

Many students report feeling frustrated in school or college. They live under the impression that they have no say in what they do and how they do things because everything they do is imposed on them. It is very likely that the indifference and passivity teachers so often complain about is at least partly the result of lack of choice.

Do you give students choices?

What are your students able to choose?

What else could your students choose if you wanted to give them more choices?

Do you think having a choice could potentially improve your students' attitude to work?

Would you be prepared to give your students more choices?

If so, what would they be?

- Give each student a worksheet and ask them to answer the questions as honestly as possible, ensuring anonymity so that nobody is worried about being criticised or punished for their opinions.

- Organise a debate and encourage people to find arguments supporting and opposing suggested changes.

- Photocopy the collated answers for each member of staff and encourage a discussion at the next staff meeting.

To have a choice or not to have a choice

What can you choose at school?

Do you think your teachers could let you have more choices?

What exactly would you LIKE to be able to choose?

Would you be more interested in your work if you had more choices?

True or false? Who knows...

The question of having, making and giving choices is probably the most controversial of all the topics in this programme.

Many of us tend to see ourselves as victims of circumstances and the thought that those circumstances could even partly be the result of our choices can make us extremely uncomfortable.

- Ask students to find a partner and decide who will be A and who B.

- Cut the page vertically in half and give one half to the A group and the other to the B group.

- Encourage students to tell their partner why they think a sentence is true or false.

- Encourage them to express their thoughts and feelings freely.

- Ask them to think of real-life examples to show which sentences are true and which are false.

- Ask students to come up with an opposite statement to the one they think is false, which will sound true to them.

- Encourage students to write their thoughts in their journals.

Do not try to establish THE TRUTH.
The statements have been designed to stimulate thinking and discussion.

True or false? Who knows...

✂

You don't get to choose the most important things in life.	Everything in my life depends on the choices I make.
On average we make one hundred choices a day.	You can choose the little things, not the important ones.
The more things there are to choose from the more difficult it gets.	It is better not to have a choice; then you don't have the problem of having to make decisions.
Every choice is a risk; whenever we make a choice we wonder what would have happened if we had made a different choice.	The most important thing you choose is your attitude. You can choose to be happy or to be miserable.
People have too many choices nowadays. That is where their problems lie.	Having no choice means having no problem.

Get inspired with quotes

Quotations are widely used to inspire, provoke deep thinking and serve as reminders of what it is we believe in.

- Make several copies of the quotation sheet and cut out individual quotations so that there is one for every student.

- Ask them to get into pairs and tell each other what the quotation means to them.

- Ask them to think of a real-life example in which this quotation would be applicable.

- Ask if they know a different quote which has the same or opposite meaning.

- Encourage them to walk around the room, look at other people's quotations and find one that they like.

- Suggest they write it in their journal and illustrate it with a picture, a collage or computer images.

- If you choose to give out the whole sheet to students, ask them to find one quote they like and one they don't like; ask them to give reasons for their dislike.

Get inspired with quotes

✂

When you know you have choices, you feel strong and in control.	We tend to resist things that have been forced upon us.
You have many more choices than you think.	When you make a choice, the responsibility is yours and there is nobody to blame.
We make a large number of choices every day and then we live with the consequences.	One of the most important choices you make is the choice of your attitude.
What you focus on, grows. You can choose what you focus on.	The pessimist sees a risk in every opportunity; the optimist sees an opportunity in every risk.
Nothing can stop someone with the right mental attitude from achieving their goal. Nothing on earth can help someone with the wrong mental attitude.	Your attitude is the force that shapes, colours and gives meaning to all your experiences in life.

A first-class tool for making choices

Edward de Bono, the creator of Lateral Thinking, designed a number of tools for developing thinking skills (De Bono, 2007). 'Plus, Minus, Interesting' is one of them.

Example
A potentially controversial statement: 'Students should choose which lessons to go to and which teachers they want to teach them.'

- Plus

  - they feel in control

  - a sense of freedom; having 'wings'

  - more enthusiasm for work

  - become really good at their best subject

- Minus

  - limited, narrow education

  - limited social life

  - overcrowded / empty classrooms

  - no challenges (for some)

- Interesting to see

  - which teachers are most popular

  - which subjects are most popular

  - how subjects go with students' personalities

  - how many people would choose not to learn anything

  - how many students choose a balanced range of subjects

- Give a few examples of some controversial statements:

  - Pupils should be able to choose what they learn at school.

  - Couples ought to be able to decide on the sex of their baby.

  - All exams should be abolished.

- Ask students to come up with other controversial statements.

- Ask students to select one they want to work with.

- Tell them to write the statement at the top of their sheet; in the boxes they write what is good about it, what is bad about it and what could be interesting about it.

A first-class tool for making choices

Your controversial proposal

+

Potential positive outcomes

Potential negative outcomes

—

?

It would be interesting to see…

Your attitude shapes and colours all your experiences

According to the *Collins English Dictionary*, 'attitude' is the way a person views something or tends to behave towards it, often in an evaluative way.

Is it at all possible to choose how we see the world and people around us, how we interpret people's behaviour? Is it possible to become more positive or more negative in our outlook, to feel differently about things?

One of the choices which has the greatest impact on life is our choice of attitude, the way we see the world and ourselves. This is because our attitude is the force that shapes, colours and gives meaning to all experience in life.

- The word 'attitude' is frequently used to mean 'bad, negative attitude'. It is important to let your students know what the word 'attitude' really means.

- Read the story 'Travellers' to your students and ask them to talk to a partner about the key message or to write in their journal what they think this story means.

- Encourage students to think about their own life experiences and remember a situation when their attitude differed from someone else's, although they were apparently experiencing the same thing.

- Ask them to write a story illustrating different attitudes towards the same experience.

Your attitude shapes and colours all your experiences

Travellers

An Old Man was sitting on a hard wooden bench waiting for his bus. He was going to Brighton to visit some friends he hadn't seen for a long time. As he was imagining the lovely day ahead of him, a Young Man approached him.

'Excuse me,' he said, 'I'm going to Brighton and I've never been there before. Do you know what it is like?'

'Where have you come from?' asked the Old Man.

'Birmingham,' said the Young Man.

'Well, what's that like?'

'Oh, it's a dreadful place, full of traffic and noise and dirt and unfriendly people.'

'I expect you will find Brighton just the same,' said the Old Man.

'Oh dear ... thanks,' said the Young Man with resignation in his voice as he walked slowly away.

A moment later another Young Man appeared and joined the Old Man on his bench.

'Excuse me,' he said, 'I'm going to Brighton and I've never been there before. Do you know what it is like?'

'Where have you come from?' asked the Old Man.

'Birmingham'.

'Well, what is that like?'

'Oh, it's a wonderful place. Full of life, excitement, colour and really friendly people,' answered the second Young Man.

'Well, I expect you will find Brighton just the same,' said the Old Man.

'Oh good, thank you,' said the Young Man and he ran to catch his bus.

The Old Man smiled and nodded his head.

Adapted from Revell and Norman, 2000

More inspiring quotes

Quotes, inspiring as they may be, often sound ambiguous and open to different interpretations. They provide good material for discussions.

Some students may find a few of the quotations difficult to understand. Choose the ones your students will understand without your help. The concepts are challenging enough and you don't want them struggling with the words on top of getting to grips with the ideas!

- Make photocopies of the quotes and give each student the whole sheet asking them to find one that speaks to them,

or

- cut out individual quotations, giving a random quote to each student.

- Ask them to get in pairs and tell each other what they think the quotation means.

- Ask them to think of a real-life example in which their quote could be applicable.

- Ask if they know a different quote which has the same / opposite meaning.

- Encourage them to walk around the room and find out what other people think about their chosen quote.

- Suggest that they write or stick the best quote in their journal and illustrate it in any way they like.

More inspiring quotes

Find the quote you like best, cut it out and glue it in your journal.

My life is to a large extent the result of all the choices I have made. I can continue making similar choices. I also have the power to make different choices.	When you feel you have no choice, you feel weak and powerless. You see yourself as a victim. When you know you have choices, you feel stronger and in control.
You don't choose all the circumstances in your life. What you can choose is the way you see and interpret the circumstances.	You can choose to feel miserable because of all the things you do NOT have and everything you are NOT. Alternatively, you can appreciate everything you do have and celebrate who you are.
Learn to make choices for yourself. If you don't make your own choices, someone else will make them for you.	You make choices every single day. And then you live with the consequences of those choices.
We tend to resist things that have been forced upon us. To do things willingly, we need to have a certain amount of choice.	Having the choice to make your own decisions may be scary. The responsibility is all yours and there is nobody to blame.

Learning: a waste of time or a valuable investment?

This activity and the two that follow focus on the ultimate choice we have, namely the choice of attitude. You may let students decide which of the three activities they want to do.

People with different mental attitudes and different beliefs may experience the same thing in very different ways.

Pretending that you believe something is true and finding arguments to support it can be very challenging. This, however, is an effective way to learn to understand other people better. This is why it is worth giving it a go.

- Divide the students into two groups and assign to each group one of the views on learning (see worksheet).

- Tell them to prepare a defence of their given part and present their argument to their opponents.

- Encourage students to record in their journal how each of the beliefs will cause people to think and act in real life.

Example
If you believed that learning was a waste of time:

– how would you feel about learning?

– what would you think when people tell you to study?

– how would you act at school?

Learning: a waste of time or a valuable investment?

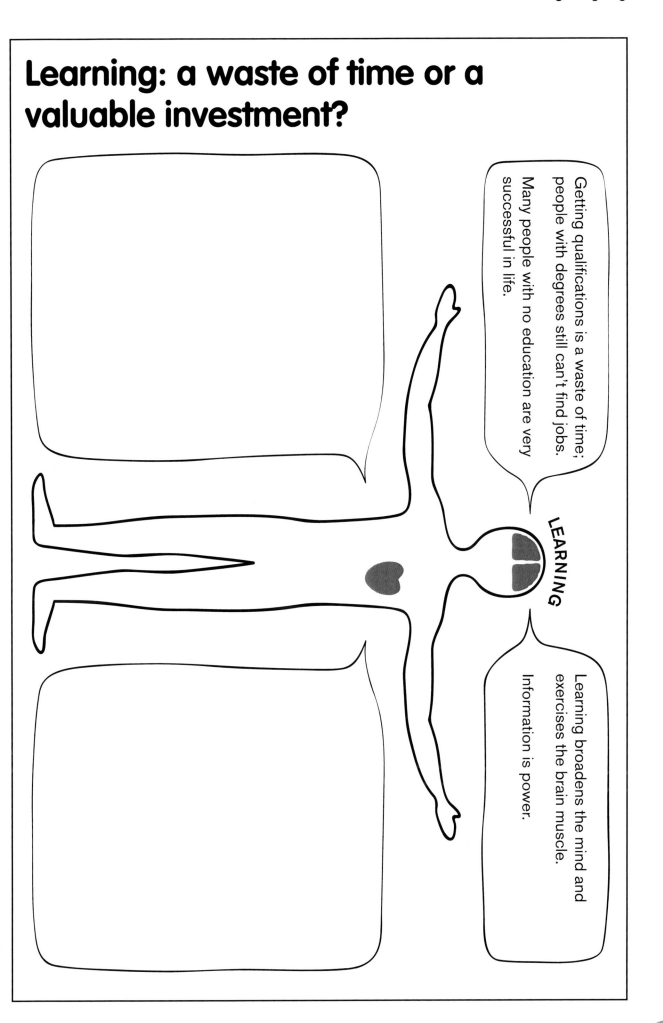

Getting qualifications is a waste of time; people with degrees still can't find jobs.

Many people with no education are very successful in life.

LEARNING

Learning broadens the mind and exercises the brain muscle.

Information is power.

Life: is it grim or 'the most precious thing'?

In life as in learning people with different kinds of attitudes and different beliefs may have dramatically different experiences of the same things. Our beliefs strongly influence our experiences of people and situations.

• Ask students to select one of the 'beliefs' on the worksheet and write:

– how people who hold those beliefs will probably act

– how people holding those beliefs will probably think and feel.

Example

Life is a series of important lessons we need to learn.

If this is your belief:

– you will probably notice when the same lesson occurs again

– you will probably choose to act in a way that will have positive consequences

– you will probably despair less when things have gone wrong

– you will probably snap out of negativity pretty quickly

– if you decide to repeat the action (the lesson) and make the same kind of choice, you will probably expect the same result

– you will probably learn that sometimes we need a number of repetitions before we learn our lesson.

Life: is it grim or 'the most precious thing'?

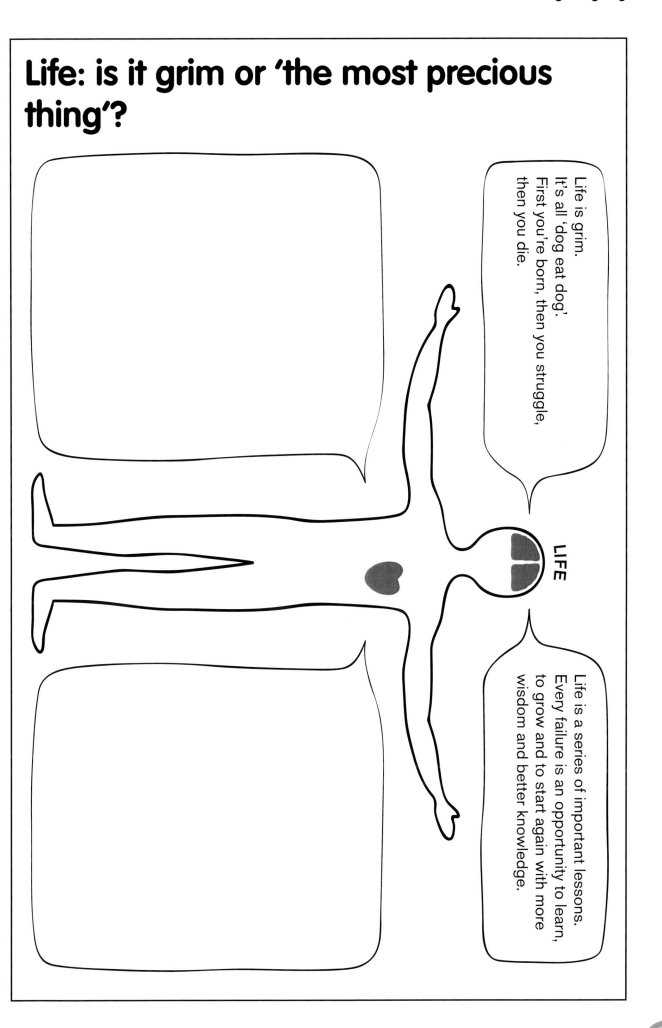

Life is grim.
It's all 'dog eat dog'.
First you're born, then you struggle,
then you die.

LIFE

Life is a series of important lessons.
Every failure is an opportunity to learn,
to grow and to start again with more
wisdom and better knowledge.

37

Victims or champions?

There are situations in life when all of us feel like powerless victims of circumstances. There are other times when we feel totally in control and on top of the world.
Each response has a payoff.

We most frequently think and act in ways that will ensure that our needs are met. When we lack confidence in our ability to handle life, we will probably think we need a great deal of help and support. Appearing weak and powerless will draw to us people ready to help. This way our need will be met.

When we wish to be seen as a strong person because we need to prove something to someone, because we need to feel good about ourselves, or because we realise that this is the right way for us to achieve our goals, we will take the driver's seat and start controlling our thoughts and actions. This way our needs will be met.

There is nothing wrong in asking for help when we need it. Some activities can only be completed in conjunction with other people.

Warning lights
Many people have a tendency to adopt one way of being (thinking, feeling and acting) most of the time. Maintaining one fixed way of seeing ourselves can have a limiting effect on the way we handle our life.

- Having introduced the topic, give out the photocopied sheets and ask students to discuss in pairs or small groups the thoughts, feelings and actions of people holding each of the beliefs.

- When enough time has been given for discussion, read out the examples below and ask students to complete their sheets.

Examples of possible responses

I blame others for what happened to me.

I hold grudges and sometimes seek revenge.

I often feel despair and tend to wallow in misery.

I spend a lot of time whining, bitching and complaining about my life.

I often assume people are out to get me.

I expect this misery to last.

Although I don't always choose what happens in my life, I do have the power to choose how I feel about it.

I know I am responsible for my life.

I tend to forgive wrongdoings and let go.

When something bad happens to me I suffer for a while but then I snap out of it, try to put the pieces together and start over.

I make an effort to look on the bright side and make the best of the situation.

I open my mind to new ideas and look for people I can trust.

I believe things will get better.

Victims or champions?

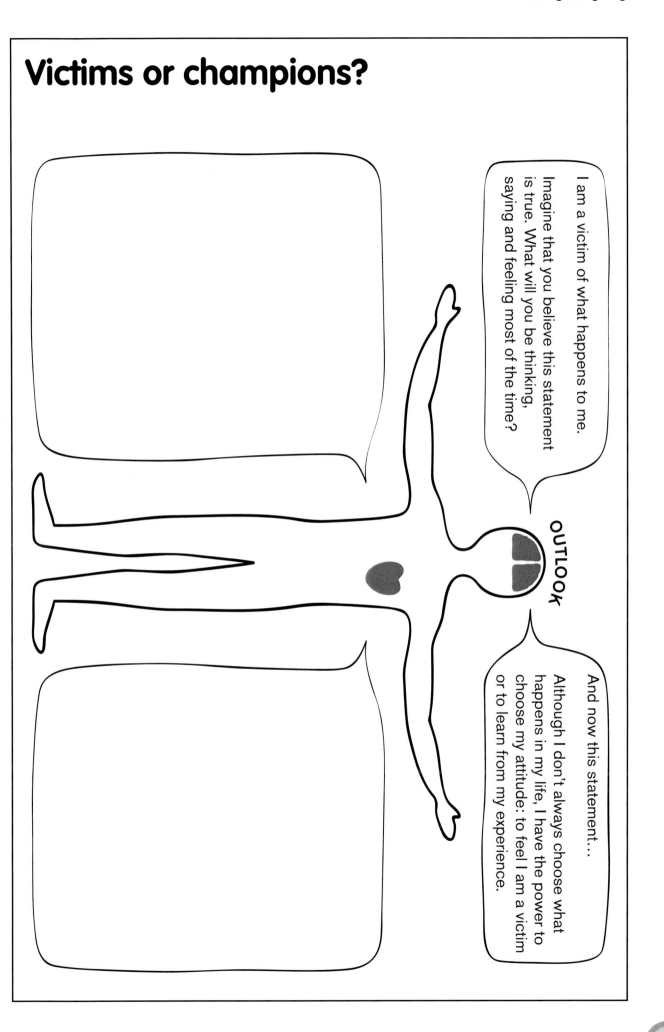

I am a victim of what happens to me. Imagine that you believe this statement is true. What will you be thinking, saying and feeling most of the time?

OUTLOOK

And now this statement...

Although I don't always choose what happens in my life, I have the power to choose my attitude: to feel I am a victim or to learn from my experience.

Awakening curiosity and interest

A curious mind is open, active and ready to learn.

Teacher's page

Born curious

Children are born learners. Young children learn a countless number of things every day, not because somebody is telling them to but because learning is as natural to them as breathing.

Why do the inborn desire to learn and natural curiosity seem to disappear once children start formal education?

- Ask students what they are curious about.

- Ask them what they were curious about when they were younger.

- Write their ideas on the board.

- Ask if they think it is easier to remember things:

  - when they want to know

  - when somebody tells them that they have to know.

Born curious

In the balloons below write things you have learnt just because you wanted to know.

Memory game

Psychological research shows that we tend to remember:

– the beginning (the first thing presented)

– the unexpected or extraordinary

– the funny

– the end (the last thing presented).

NB We also remember:

– the familiar

– something that touches our feelings

– the things associated with something we already know.

If this game proves the memory theory to be right, the words remembered by the greatest number of students will be 'holidays', 'Manchester United', 'gobbledegook' and 'shapes'.

Will this influence the way you plan your lessons?

Change the words if you think the above ones are not appropriate. Be sure to include in your list words that are unexpected, funny or amusing.

- Tell students they are about to play a memory game. Tell them to listen to a list of words.

- Read out the following words clearly, making a very short pause after each word: holidays * friends * games * fun * Manchester United * beach * boat * sand * gobbledegook * words * numbers * shapes.

- Ask the students to write down the words they remember on the photocopied sheets.

- When you see they have finished say 'Raise your hand if you have written "holidays"'.

- Count the number of hands and write it down.

- Then ask 'Who has written "friends"?' Again count the number of people and write it down. Do this with all the words.

- Whether the experiment proves the theory or not, share with students what people tend to remember.

- Tell them to plan their work as follows: as we remember things at the beginning and at the end, take frequent breaks so that you have many beginnings and many endings.

Memory game

The words you can remember:

What have you learnt about memory?

Make them laugh

Laughter is important for the learning process. It stimulates the brain's limbic system, which is said to be responsible for long-term memory.

Laughter also reduces the levels of cortisol, a stress hormone; this is important because stress is known to account for a high percentage of all learning difficulties.

Some people are naturally funny. Those of us who are not may need to introduce humour by:

– showing funny video clips

– encouraging students to tell jokes

– loosening up!

• Discuss the importance of fun and laughter in the classroom to find out more about what students think.

• Ask them to talk about things that make them laugh.

• Encourage students to think of specific jokes, songs, actors, film clips and amusing situations, and write them on their worksheets.

• Get them to write their ideas on sticky labels and stick the notes on a flip-chart.

As some wise people say, education is far too important to be taken seriously!

Make them laugh

What makes you laugh? Give as many examples as you can.

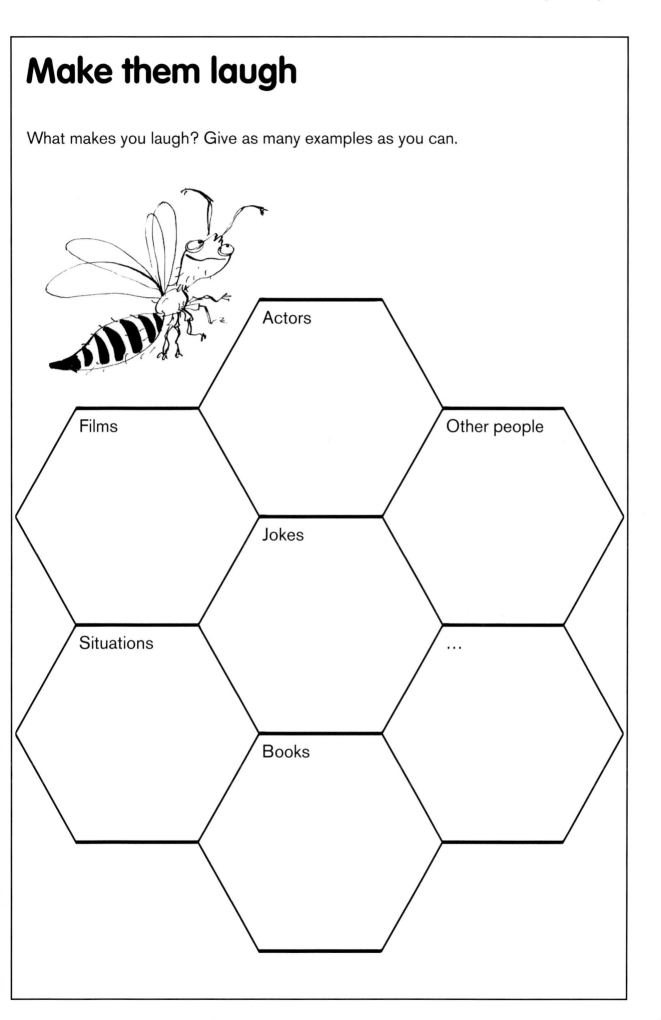

Actors

Films

Other people

Jokes

Situations

...

Books

Mystery and suspense

Monotony and predictability result in boredom and withdrawal of attention, and as the brain can never be idle, we venture into our 'dream world'. In contrast, elements of mystery, novelty and something unexpected hardly ever fail to awaken our interest and a certain level of excitement; we simply want to know.

Create a list of things that make your own teaching interesting for you, or things that could make it more interesting for your students.

1. ....

2. ....

3. ....

4. ....

5. ....

Encourage students to act in novel ways. Surprise them with something new: a hands-on task they have never done, the clothes you wear, a different tone of voice, new seating arrangements. Anything out of the ordinary, anything different from the normal routine.

NB Having to sit away from friends with classmates they hardly know, and maybe don't even like, can awaken a whole range of emotions in your students. You may want to discuss this with them.

- Ask students what makes a lesson interesting.

- If necessary, explore the meaning of the suggestions listed on the worksheet.

- Encourage students to share their thoughts with a friend.

Mystery and suspense

What makes you interested (less bored...) in class?

Put these in order from the most to the least effective:

Surprises

Extraordinary things and facts

Variety

Challenges

Things about you

Practical, hands-on activities

Investigations

1 ....

2 ....

3 ....

4 ....

5 ....

6 ....

7 ....

Which of these do you experience at school?

Be inspiring

What specifically do *you* do to get a group's attention and awaken their interest?

Jot down a few examples. Be as specific as possible.

- Make a list of three topics students have already been taught, write them on the worksheet and make copies.

- Ask students to form groups of four, give a photocopied sheet to each group and ask them to choose one of the topics for their presentations.

- Ask each group to prepare two presentations:

  – one to show how to grab attention and make the lesson really interesting,

  – another to show what to do so that students immediately lose interest, feel bored and disengaged.

- Suggest they start by putting all their ideas on a large sheet of paper – write, make pictures/ scribbles, make a story-board, a mind map – anything to illustrate as many ideas as the group can come up with.

- Organise a show of all presentations and, if possible, record them on video.

- Show the video to teachers in the next staff meeting (optional!).

 The adolescent brain is fascinated by novelty and emotion.

Be inspiring

Choose one topic from the list below.

1 ....

2 ....

3 ....

If you were a teacher, how could you make the topic really boring?

How could you make the topic really interesting?

Orchestrated learning

Benefits of the activity:

- Students have a choice of questions.

- They focus on something that interests them, something they want to know.

- They experience multi-sensory learning:

  - visual (reading and looking at pictures)

  - kinaesthetic (standing, walking while speaking)

  - auditory (listening to explanations, hearing themselves speak).

- Repetition enables students to remember information.

- The activity can be:

  - used to introduce a new topic

  - used as a revision tool, provided there is some new information and both questions and answers are presented in a way that awakens interest

  - made up by students themselves (with the teacher checking the answers before the group plays the game).

The example of an orchestrated learning activity on p53 comes from *Introducing Children to their Amazing Brains* by Eva Hoffman (2002).

- Think of some truly interesting questions about your topic (twice as many questions as there are students in your group).

- Divide an A4 sheet into two parts and on each half type one question.

- Prepare answers to the questions and illustrate them with pictures / graphs.

- Divide a second A4 sheet into two parts and type one answer in each section.

- Photocopy questions and answers on paper of two different colours.

- Put questions and answers back to back and laminate each Q & A individually.

- Display all cards (questions up) on the table and ask each student to choose a question that interests them and think about possible answers to it.

- When all students have their cards in front of them, ask them to turn over and read the answers on the back.

- Ask students to pair up and share with their partners what they have learnt.

- Encourage students to change partners three or four times.

Orchestrated learning

Why is setting goals important for learning?

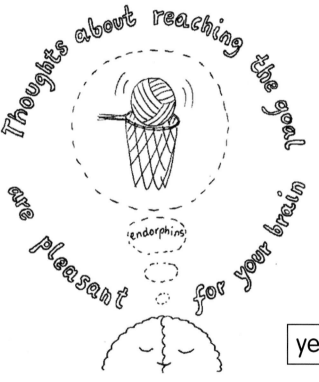

Thoughts about achieving what you want to achieve produce 'feel good' chemicals called *endorphins*.

They make you feel good and work with enthusiasm.

yes!

Start each work session by thinking that what you will learn will help you:

* be smarter

* get good grades

* feel good about yourself.

Hoffman, 2002; © Justina Langley

Teacher or entertainer?

Teachers who know how to entertain students are almost always sure to get their message across.

Some teachers say that it is not their job to make learning interesting. In their opinion they are supposed to teach their subject and not to entertain their audience.

Are they right or wrong? What do you think?

 Open your mind and be prepared to listen.

• Make students feel at ease and tell them that only honest comments are going to be helpful to them and to you.

• Encourage discussions in groups.

• Give each group a large sheet of paper and ask for comments, pictures, collages on the subject.

• Ask each group to write their comments on the worksheet.

• Let students decide whether they want to present their comments as individuals or as groups.

Teacher or entertainer?

Answer the questions honestly. Be specific when giving examples but avoid using names.

Think about a lesson that you found tedious and boring. What did the teacher do that made your brain switch off?

Think about a lesson that you found interesting and fun. What did the teacher do to get your attention and interest?

The secret

Nothing triggers our curiosity more effectively than when someone tells us they know a secret but won't share it. The moment we are not supposed to know something, we experience a burning desire to find out what it is.

A book written by Rhonda Byrne is entitled *The Secret* **(Byrne, 2008). Does the title intrigue you? Would you like to know what secret the author is talking about? Would you be inclined to buy it / read it / ask somebody what it is about?**

Here are a couple of quotations from *The Secret*. **Read them to your students and inspire a discussion.**

> *Everything that's coming into your life you are attracting into your life. And it's attracted to you by virtue of the images you're holding in your mind. It's what you're thinking. Whatever is going on in your mind you are attracting to you.*
>
> Bob Proctor (The Secret DVD)

> *The Law of Attraction is forming your entire experience and this all-powerful law is doing that through your thoughts.*
>
> Rhonda Byrne

Those who would like to know more can visit the website www.thesecret.tv

- Ask students to remember a situation when someone was hiding something from them.

- Encourage them to share how this made them feel and whether they tried to do something to find out.

- Show your students the illustration overleaf and ask what they think is the most important thing people want to know.
Accept all answers.

The secret

Two tips to awaken curiosity

Tip 1 Ask more – tell less

'Asking' does not have to mean testing what students know. Whenever possible ask genuine questions, questions to which you yourself don't know the answer or all the answers.

Here are some types of questions that may be successful in stimulating interest:

– Have you ever experienced …?

– Who can guess …?

– Can you think of three possible answers to …?

– What could happen if …?

– In what situation would … be a good solution?

– What are the possible ways of …?

This way all answers have validity and all students are encouraged to think and respond without the fear (often paralysing!) of making mistakes.

Something for you to do

Think of a topic you have just taught or one you are about to explore with your students and write a list of questions with the potential to awaken their curiosity.

1 ....

2 ....

3 ....

4 ....

5 ....

Their feedback could be most valuable!

Teacher's
page

Tip 2 Add seasoning

Spice up your lessons with some extraordinary or amazing facts, ideas, discoveries.

1 Give your students an unconventional task for homework: tell them to find some extraordinary information connected with the subject and have each student present the result of their search to the class.

2 Ask them to find some extraordinarily interesting things connected with your subject:

– on the internet

– in magazines

– in TV / radio programmes

– from friends and colleagues you can enlist to help

– from books which are compilations of interesting, amazing things

– …………………………..?

3 Tell students to collect all the information in a special portfolio – it will be there ready for use whenever you need it.

Say to them, 'Start your portfolio of amazing facts today!'

- The human heart creates enough pressure while pumping to squirt blood a distance of 30 feet.

- It's impossible to sneeze with your eyes open.

- On average Americans eat 18 acres of pizza every day.

- In ancient Egypt, priests plucked every hair from their bodies, including their eyebrows and eyelashes.

- Any number squared is equal to one more than the numbers on either side of it –
5 x 5 is 25, 4 x 6 is 24 etc.

- The king of hearts is the only king without a moustache.

- No piece of square dry paper can be folded in half more than seven times.

- A crocodile cannot stick its tongue out.

More tips to awaken curiosity

Tip 1 Give choices

Find out what students *would like* to know.

Imagine the following scenario: you have just had a lovely lunch at home when a friend comes and invites you to have a snack in a Chinese restaurant nearby. You are polite and do not want to hurt your friend's feelings so you reluctantly accept the invitation. The problem is that you are not hungry! You don't feel like going out! And most importantly, you really hate Chinese food!

Isn't this exactly what we do to our students in the way we attempt to educate them? And then we are surprised that they rebel!

Try doing the following:

– Give your students an overview of the topic (including all the sub-topics) you are planning to teach.

– Tell them a little about each sub-topic and make it sound exciting, using your 'interesting facts' portfolio.

– Ask everybody to choose a sub-topic they would like to know more about (or at least something that sounds remotely interesting to them).

– Ask students to find as much information as they can about their chosen area and bring the results of their search to class.

– Collect the papers to check whether the information is correct.

– Give back the papers and organise peer teaching sessions. You may be amazed how much they will learn.

Tip 2 Design games

1a A topic-related word puzzle

- Give students a list of words connected with the topic you have just taught.

- Tell students to create a crossword puzzle with all the words given and include a few words of their own choice.

- Collect all puzzles and check the clues for accuracy.

- Organise swapping the puzzles and give students enough time to solve them.

Try to ensure that everyone experiences success.

1b A topic-related puzzle designed by you (an alternative form of assessment)

- Design a puzzle yourself and use it as a form of revision or assessment. It may seem like a lot of work, but once you have it done, it can be used over and over again.

2 A topic-related board game (suitable for homework)

- Give students a topic or a list of topics which develop in a linear way, eg a historical event, a science process, a biography, a story / a play.

- Get students to form groups and ask each group to design a board game, including an illustrated board and detailed written instructions.

- Give students time to play a board game designed by another group.

Benefits of the games:

- Games provide an alternative form of learning and revising.

- They encourage self-directed learning, searching for information, and give students feedback on their performance.

- They encourage peer teaching and team work.

- They provide an alternative way to assess students' learning.

Nurturing dreams and setting goals

Goals are dreams with a timescale.

Promises, promises
Prepare for setting goals

Some children know quite early in life what they want to be when they grow up, others take a little longer, still others … much longer!

Before we start making big plans for the future it is a good idea to learn to keep promises.

- Tell students that whether they already have plans for their future or not, it is necessary to start by learning to keep promises.

- Ask students what promises they make and to write them on the board.

  – I will play with you tomorrow.

  – I will bring you some stickers / a CD / a DVD.

  – I will be back in 10 minutes.

  – I will wash up all my dirty cups.

  – I will feed the cat every night.

  – I will eat fewer sweets.

- Ask them why they sometimes fail to keep their promises.

  – I get too tired.

  – I forget.

  – I feel lazy.

  – I think that it's not so important and that I can do it later.

  – I think 'just one more …'

- Ask students what they could do to be better at keeping their promises.

  – Write things down.

  – Set an alarm clock to remind them.

  – Reward themselves for keeping the promise.

  – Ask someone to remind them.

  – Remember how they feel when someone breaks a promise they have made to them.

Promises, promises
Prepare for setting goals

Do you make promises similar to those listed below?
If so, tick the ones you make most often.

☐ I will call you tomorrow.

☐ I will clean up the mess when I get back.

☐ I will text you in 10 minutes.

☐ I will return your CD on Sunday.

☐ I will not eat chocolate for a week.

☐ I will walk my dog every night, whatever the weather!

Do you always keep your promises?
If not, what are your excuses?

....

....

....

....

Would any of these be your excuses?

- You forget
- You succumb to temptation.
- You think: well, just one more time …
- You think: not today!
- You think: it doesn't REALLY matter.
- You think: they can wait another day.

Commit to your promise

**An important step towards setting and
achieving life goals is to start noticing the
promises we make and then get into the
habit of keeping them.**

- Ask students to think about some promises
  they want to learn to keep.

- Tell them to make a promise to do something
  for a short time, one to five days will be
  enough.

  - For three days I will wash up after dinner.

  - I will pack my school bag the night before for
    five days.

- Tell them to think of ways to make it easier for
  themselves.

  - Write their promise down where they can
    see it.

  - Tell somebody about their promise.

  - Ask someone to remind them.

 Keep your promise when you've made it or don't make a promise at all.

Commit to your promise

My promise to myself:

Signed

Date

My perfect day

According to the psychologist Raj Persaud, describing our ideal day may give us an idea what it is that we really like, possibly what it is we want to do in life (Persaud, 2006).

When asked to describe their ideal day, people often paint a picture of time with no obligations, just fun; doing only what they love doing.

- Ask students to draw a picture of their best day and include all the things they would like to do that day; instead of drawing they may choose to make a collage, cut out photographs from magazines, make a mind map, etc.

- Accept all ideas students may have, strongly resisting any form of evaluation or judgment.

- Ask students whether their 'perfect day' would be different if they were to live this way for the rest of their life.

- Discuss with students the positive and negative consequences of living this kind of life.

My perfect day

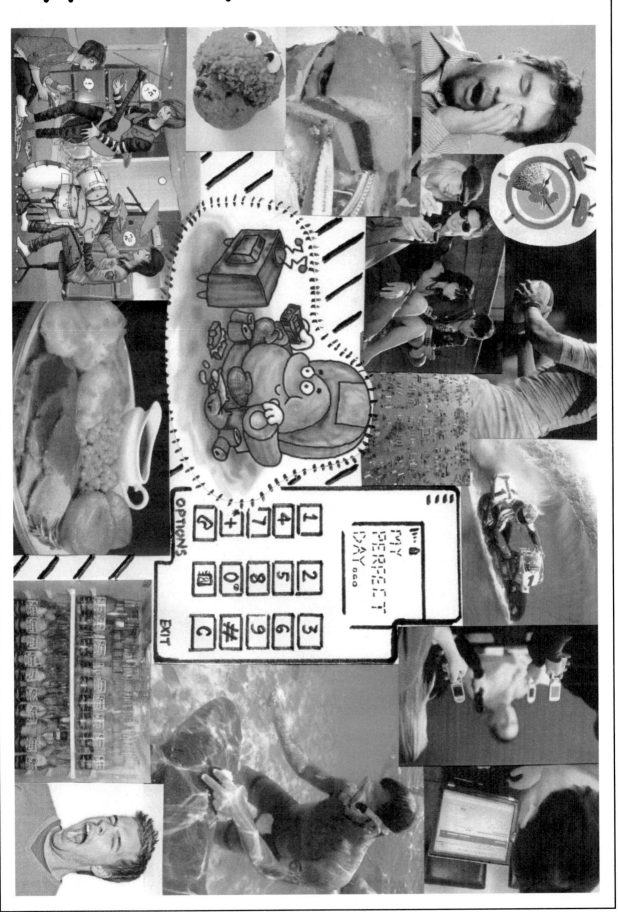

Your very own goals

There are different categories of goals, all of them valid and all of them important. People have different goals which may depend on their age, sex, social class, culture, family tradition and other factors.

What teenagers tend to want:
friends, a new mobile phone, a big room, a lot of money, a sports car, holidays with friends, a horse and stables, to be a celebrity, fancy technological devices, CDs and DVDs.

People in their twenties and thirties often want:
a big house, a new car, holidays in the Bahamas, beautiful clothes, a good-looking boyfriend / a beautiful girlfriend, a lovely family, a good job, a healthy bank account, esteem of peers, a position of power.

Later in life people may want:
to give and receive love, to feel needed, to make a difference, to be happy and spread happiness, to have enough money, to experience a sense of fulfilment, to do something meaningful for others.

- Tell students that what people want in life varies from person to person and often changes as they get older.

- Ask them to think how people's goals change as they get older.

- Ask them to think what their goals are right now, eg:

  – What do you want to possess?
  property, clothes, equipment

  – What do you want to achieve?
  fame, interesting profession, well-paid job

  – How do you want to feel about yourself?
  content with life, excited

  – What kind of person do you want to be?
  a kind friend, a caring son or daughter, a responsible student, a layabout

  – How do you want to make a difference?
  support charity, voluntary work
  help in elderly care homes, recycle

Your very own goals

Put a few goals in each net. Start with the suggestions below and if you wish add some of your own. Some goals may belong to more than one category.

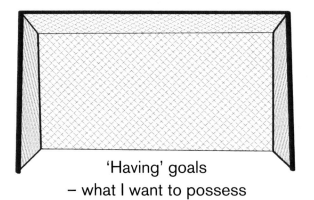

'Having' goals
– what I want to possess

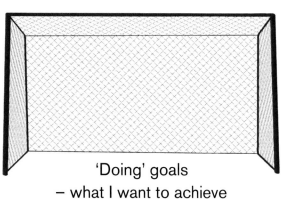

'Doing' goals
– what I want to achieve

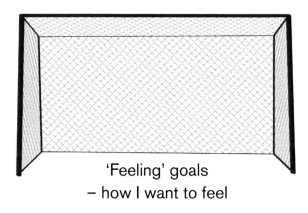

'Feeling' goals
– how I want to feel

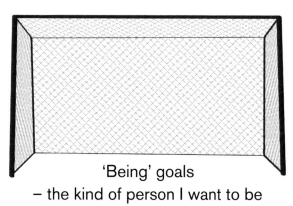

'Being' goals
– the kind of person I want to be

1. to have a good job

2. to be helpful to my friends

3. to be really happy

4. to have a fast car and a big house

5. to be working for a charity

6. to feel valued

7. to earn a good salary

8. to feel loved by someone special

9. to make someone happy

10. to feel important

11. to become a celebrity

12. to do something for my community / the world

13. to have a family

14. to have good qualifications

If you could only have three goals in life, what would they be?

Thinking small or thinking big

Notice the students who do not have a goal and those who don't want to set goals for fear of failure. This activity is particularly for them.

Sometimes 'thinking small' may be better than 'thinking big'.

Very many people never think about their goals; they don't make long-term plans but take things as they come. We all know someone living a successful and happy life who did not set big goals in their youth.

Big goals can be scary. Sometimes we may not want to dream in case we fail to make the dream come true – the pain of disappointment would be too much to bear.

Example
Goal: to play the electric guitar and have a band

Breaking it into small goals:
1 Buy or borrow an instrument.
2 Find a teacher or a friend who can help you learn some chords.
3 Learn to read tabs (using the internet).
4 Practise an hour a day.
5 Listen to some bands and learn some songs.
6 Ask around for people who might want to play with you.

- Reassure the students who say that they don't have any goals by telling them about people who didn't have goals and yet live happy and successful lives.

- Tell them that dreaming big may not be suitable for everybody and that for many the way forward is setting very small goals, goals they are sure they can achieve.

- Suggest they think about the question 'If you did have a goal, what would it be?' and ask them to write two or three possible goals, all *very small* and easily *achievable*.

- It may be right to leave it at that; however, if you see that students are coming up with ideas, take it a step further and ask whether they could be prepared to set these goals for themselves.

- Tread gently and don't expect immediate results.

- Encourage students to make collages, internet images or drawings which represent their hypothetical goals.

- If possible, give your students John Bird's (founder of *The Big Issue*) little book *How to Change Your Life in 7 Steps* and suggest they read the first few pages.

Thinking small or thinking big

IF I HAD A GOAL, it would be:

Break your goal down into a few small and easily achievable goals.
Write or draw the small goals in the segments of the circle.

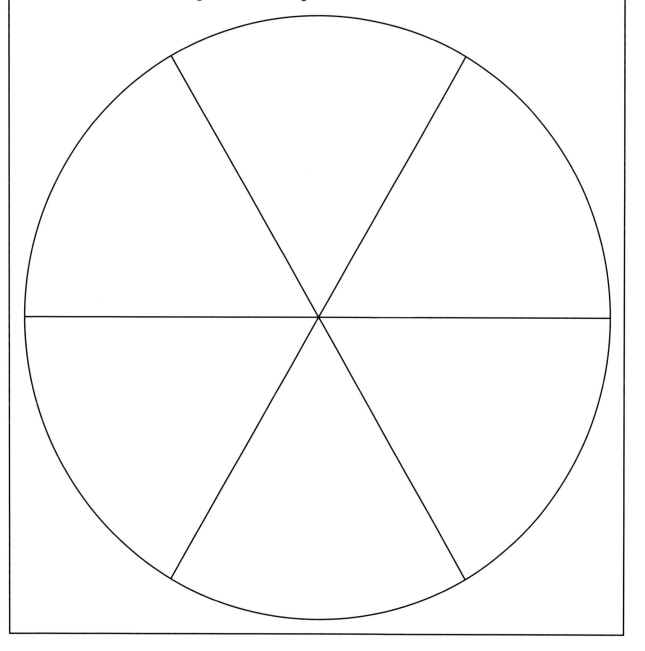

Teacher's page

365 steps towards your goal

If we make a habit of taking action towards our goal every day it will get easier and easier to do because anything we do repeatedly becomes a habit.

If we decide to take just one single step a day towards our goal, imagine how much closer to our goal we will be in a year? 365 steps closer!

- Encourage students to buy a small diary and every day write in it what action they have taken towards their goal.

- Tell them that recording every step taken towards their goal will make it more tangible and will serve as a constant reminder. They will enjoy looking back and seeing how far they have come.

How can you eat an elephant?

One bite at a time

365 steps towards your goal

Buy yourself a small diary, one that will easily slip into your pocket or a bag, and record every little step you make towards your goal.

Sort out your life

Not many people develop a habit of stopping to think what it is that they really want in life and what it is they don't want.

This kind of awareness exercise will help young people make this important realisation and help them see the benefit of developing the habit of reflecting on their values and goals.

- Ask students to assign each statement to the column that seems most appropriate. Then encourage them to add their own ideas to the columns.

- Alternatively, ask them to come up with their ideas, then give out the worksheets and ask them to choose anything relevant to them and add it to their own lists.

Sort out your life

What is it that I really want?

I don't want to…   I would like to…

☒ ....   ☑ ....

☒ ....   ☑ ....

☒ ....   ☑ ....

☒ ....   ☑ ....

☒ ....   ☑ ....

☒ ....   ☑ ....

- resist peer pressure

- feel that I am worse than others

- trust myself

- have life goals

- be over-concerned about what others think

- appreciate who I am and what I have

- wear myself out

- cave in under peer pressure

- take care of my health

- act arrogantly to hide my insecurities

It isn't a goal unless...

It is necessary to differentiate between goals and wishful thinking.

1 A goal has to be *specific*.
A goal: I will learn five new French words every day for a month.
A wish: I want to improve my French.

2 A goal must be *measurable*.
A goal: I will exercise three times a week for 30 minutes.
A wish: I want to do more exercise.

3 A goal must be *time-related*.
A goal: I will learn to play this guitar piece by next Sunday.
A wish: I want to learn to play this guitar piece.

4 A goal must be *positive*.
A goal: I will eat sugar-free foods for three weeks.
A wish: I want to cut down on sweets.

5 A goal must be *personal*.
A goal: I will take the dog for a walk every night for three months.
A wish: I want my brother to take the dog for a walk.

6 A goal can be very ambitious but needs to be *achievable*.
A goal: I will run the London marathon next year.
A wish: Although I am 65, I want to become an Olympic champion.

- Give students the mind map and go through the goal-setting rules with them.

- Write on the board some examples of incorrectly formulated goals and ask students what is wrong with them.

- Get students to formulate the goals correctly.

- Encourage students to think of a goal for themselves.

Examples
– Every day for one month I will read, mind map and memorise two pages of my science revision book.

– I will learn to play three songs on my guitar by the end of next week.

– For three months (apart from birthdays and other special celebrations) I will eat only healthy food.

- Tell students to represent their goal in a picture, collage or graph. The more detailed they make it, the more likely they are to keep working towards it.

It isn't a goal unless...

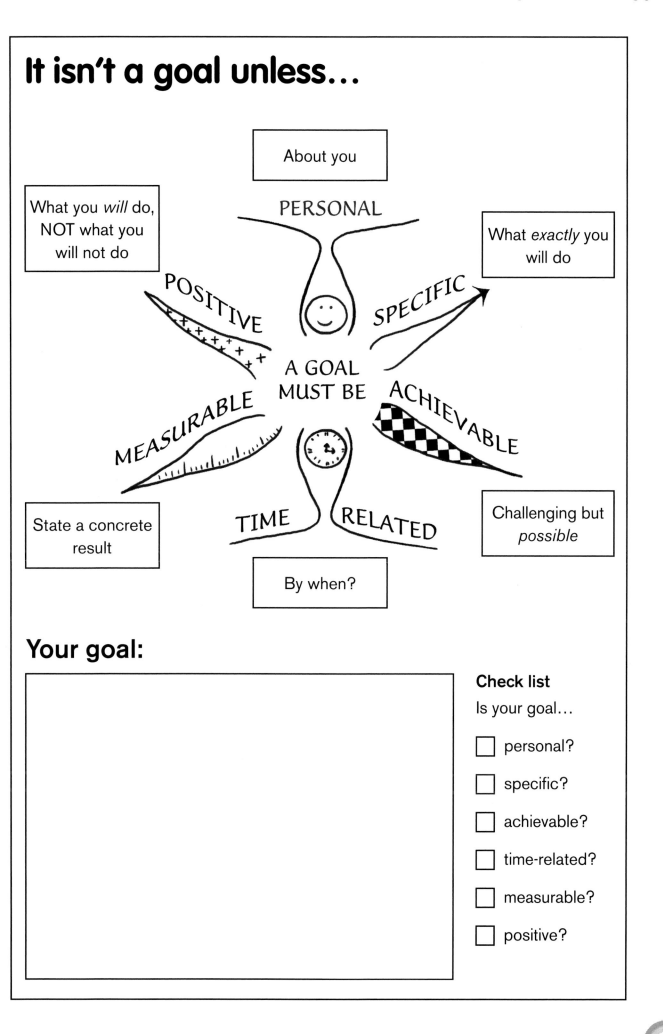

About you

PERSONAL

What you *will* do, NOT what you will not do

What *exactly* you will do

POSITIVE

SPECIFIC

A GOAL MUST BE

MEASURABLE

ACHIEVABLE

State a concrete result

TIME RELATED

Challenging but *possible*

By when?

Your goal:

Check list

Is your goal…

☐ personal?

☐ specific?

☐ achievable?

☐ time-related?

☐ measurable?

☐ positive?

Your goal in colour

Brian Mayne has created a programme in which he teaches people about the importance of setting goals and encourages them to represent their goals in a pictorial form (Mayne, 2006). He stresses that goals represented as colourful pictures are more likely to be realised than those expressed in words: people identify with them and remember them better.

- Hand out the worksheets and give students the following instructions:

  – In the large oval draw your biggest current goal; use colours and make it look attractive.

  – In the smaller oval shapes draw goals that will support your main goal.

  – On the lines on one side of the time-trunk write what help and support you will need to achieve your goal.

  – On the lines on the opposite side write the names of people or organisations you will approach to get the support you need.

  – Add more lines if necessary.

  – At the bottom of the time-trunk write today's date; at the top write the date by which you will achieve your goal.

Your goal in colour

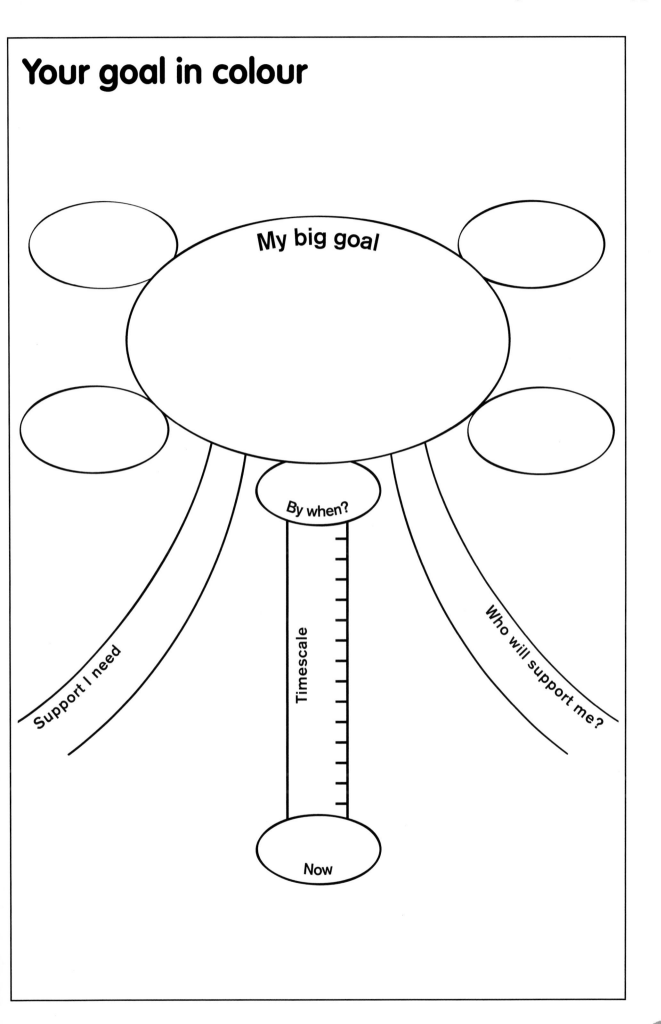

Who's in charge?

For most of us, there are times when we feel our life is on automatic pilot.

From morning till night we go about our business moving from one thing to another, never stopping to think, to take a breath, to just be.

Psychologists, therapists, philosophers and other wise people tell us to live consciously.

What does 'living consciously' actually mean to you?

It includes ensuring that every day you:

– remember the really important things in life

– take time to think about where your life is going

– take time to be still and listen to your intuition

– plan your future and become truly responsible for what happens in your life.

- Photocopy the sheet for every student and then ask them to choose the quotation they like best and glue it in their journal.

- Encourage students to make posters as reminders.

- Tell students they could turn their posters into postcards and send them to friends and family.

- You could also put the quotes on PowerPoint and play some relaxing instrumental music while showing them.

Who's in charge?

If you don't know where you are going, how will you know when you get there?	You are the main character in your own life story. Write it well.
This is not a rehearsal. This is your life and you're living it now.	Today is the first day of the rest of my life. How will I choose to live it?
Only those who have a dream can make their dream come true.	To accomplish great things we must dream as well as act.
A goal will give you a direction, something worth striving for, a track to get back to when you feel lost.	Every journey begins with a decision to make the first step in a chosen direction.
How could you eat an elephant? One bite at a time!	If you don't have your own goals, you will spend your life working to achieve the goals of others.
Having a vision of what you want to achieve in life is the key to a successful and fulfilling life.	Nothing you experience and learn when pursuing a goal is ever wasted. No matter whether you succeed or not, you learn what works and what doesn't.

Teacher's
page

Rocks, pebbles and sand

Nothing we have experienced and learnt when pursuing a goal is ever wasted, no matter whether we have or have not succeeded in achieving it. We have learnt what works and what doesn't.

Talk to students about goals. A *rock* in this story is your vision, your big dream, a kind of life you want for yourself. It is about the person you want to be and the things you want to achieve for yourself and for others.

A *pebble* symbolises every big step forward that may bring you closer to your big dream, eg moving to another country or another town, getting the right qualifications or some necessary experience. Pebbles are also all the things you consider important.

***Sand* represents the many rather insignificant things we do. They may sometimes be pleasant but have no link with our life vision.**

- Read the story to your students or ask them to read it to themselves.

- Encourage them to talk about the meaning of rocks, pebbles and sand.

- Ask students whether they have already found out what their 'rocks, pebbles and sand' are.

Rocks, pebbles and sand

The jar

One morning Nathan woke up very early. For some reason he was feeling anxious and troubled about his life and his future. Nathan soon realised there was no chance he would go back to sleep, so he decided to go for a walk along the beach in the hope that this would help clear his head. He walked slowly, breathing in the fresh sea air and enjoying the feeling of the sand under his bare feet. Suddenly he noticed an old man who was sitting on a rock and picking up stones and pebbles from the shore.

As Nathan approached, the old man looked at Nathan's face.

'What is troubling you, young man?' he asked.

A little taken aback, Nathan thought for a moment and said slowly, looking into the old man's eyes, 'I don't know what to do with my life and this is bothering me a great deal.'

The old man picked up a large jar that had been washed up by the sea. He then filled the jar with large rocks and turned to Nathan.

'Is the jar full?'

'It certainly is,' Nathan replied.

The old man picked a handful of small pebbles and put them into the jar, watching them roll into the spaces between the rocks. He then turned again to Nathan.

'Now is the jar full?'

Nathan smiled and nodded.

Once more the old man reached down, picked up a handful of sand and poured it into the jar. This time there was no space left in the jar.

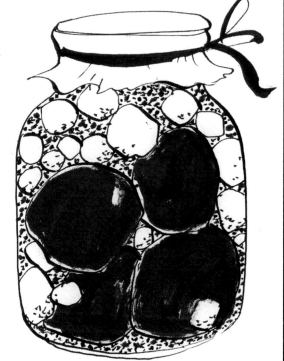

'You see, the rocks represent the most important things in a person's life such as family, partner, children, health, spirituality, knowledge, wisdom. The pebbles represent other things that matter to people, things like money, jobs, houses, clothes. The sand is everything else, things that don't really matter.

'Some people,' continued the old man, 'make the mistake of putting the sand into the jar first and then there is no space left for the important things, no room for the pebbles and certainly not for the rocks.'

'Thank you for your wisdom,' said Nathan as he picked up a couple of rocks and went on his way.

Slogging, slacking and prioritising

Slogging
(all *rocks* and *pebbles*, no *sand*)
There are young people who seem to be totally devoted to their work. They:

– study

– help others learn

– earn money

– care for others

– achieve their goals

– take on other people's problems.

Slacking
(all *sand*, no *rocks* or *pebbles*)
There are young people who seem to be permanently glued to the small screen. All their time is spent:

– watching TV

– playing games

– chatting on the phone for hours

– sleeping

– surfing the net

– hanging around.

Prioritising
(*rocks* first, then *pebbles* and *sand*)
There are young people who have found the right balance in life. They have identified their rocks, pebbles and sand, and have made prioritising a habit. They start with rocks, then deal with pebbles and make time for some sand.

• Ask students to identify rocks, pebbles and sand on the worksheet.

• Encourage group discussion – this will help students see that their priorities may differ.

• Tell them to make their own lists and identify:

– their sand

– their pebbles

– their rocks.

Plan to start with the rocks, then do the rest.

Slogging, slacking and prioritising

Here is what one student said he needed to do. Decide which are ROCKS, PEBBLES and SAND and write letters R, P or S next to each item.

	Buy a pair of trainers
	Call a friend
	Return a DVD
	Prepare for tomorrow's science test
	Practise the piano
	Walk down the high street
	Meet a mate
	Help Mum with housework
	Surf the net
	Learn about a new computer program
	Watch a favourite TV programme

Now make your own list of things you need / want to do and indicate which are Rocks, which Pebbles and which Sand.

Living your dream

As children and teenagers we spend a lot of time dreaming about our future lives. Then comes LIFE and we stop dreaming…

Take this opportunity to start dreaming again. Rekindle the dreams of your youth or begin to dream new dreams.

You are truly alive as long as you can still dream.

The collage overleaf is an example of a student's dream life.

- Tell students to describe their dream life and remind them to include all kinds of goals.

- Suggest they include the following:
  - what they want to have
  - what kind of person they want to be
  - how they want to feel
  - what they want to achieve.

- Tell them they may draw a picture, make a collage, make a mind map or simply write.

- Ask them:

  'What will you need to do for the dream to come true?'

Living your dream

Values and priorities

Our values are our life guides. How we live our life depends largely on our priorities, which stem from our values.

Examples of values people may hold:

– **fairness and honesty**

– **appreciation and gratitude**

– **responsibility**

– **financial success**

– **loyalty and respect**

– **service and work**

– **kindness**

– **freedom**

Examples of priorities:

– **family**

– **friendships**

– **house**

– **education**

– **work**

– **money**

– **interests (write what they are)**

– **things, possessions**

– **helping others**

– **confidence**

- Explain the meaning of *values* and give a couple of examples. Then ask students to come up with more examples and write them on the board.

- Ask them to identify their most important *values* and ask them to record them in the inner ring.

- Ask students to identify the *important* things in their lives (their priorities) and write them in the outer ring.

Values and priorities

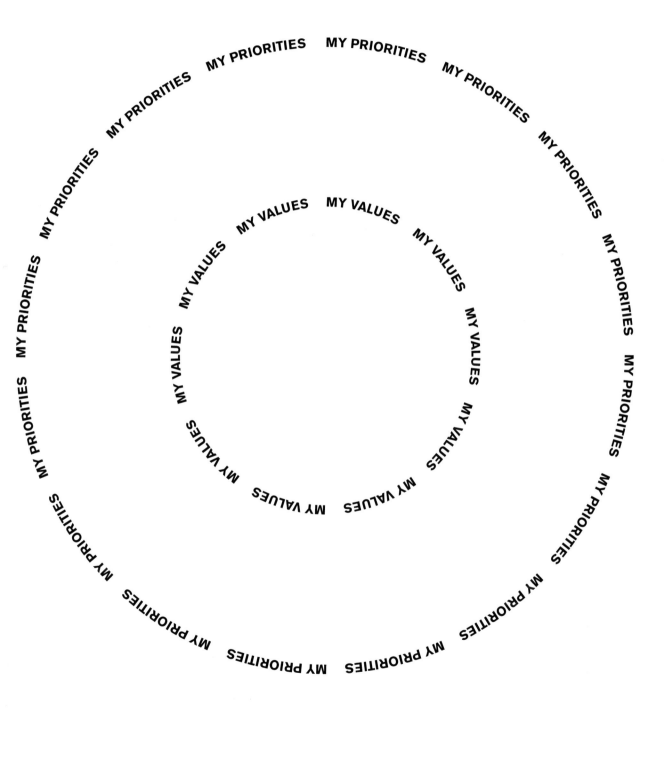

Change of direction

Failing to achieve a goal can be a very traumatic experience. When we have put a lot of effort and hopes into something that didn't work out, we are likely to feel disheartened and demoralised.

'Pick yourself up, brush yourself off, start all over again' go the words of a song... often easier said than done.

Our effort is never wasted! We learn from everything we do so that we can do it better next time. When we strive to achieve a worthwhile goal, we develop as a person; we learn about hard work, about discipline and resilience, all of which will make us better equipped to live a fulfilling life.

We need to learn to treat all failure as feedback and to find out what lessons we need to learn. It may take time, effort and possibly some help from someone caring and wise.

When we have learnt our lessons, when we recover from the disappointment, we can either rethink our strategies or change our direction.

- Hand out the worksheet and ask students what they think it means.

- Tell students: 'When climbing towards your goal, as you go higher and higher, your horizons expand. You begin to see different things and your whole perspective changes.'

- Reassure students that although it is possible that they will still choose to pursue their present life goal, it is also possible that they will decide to go in another direction.

- Tell your students about the people you know who changed their direction and for whom it was the right decision.

Additional discussion questions:

– Have you ever experienced a change of direction?

– Why did you make your decision to drop your original goal?

– Was it a good decision?

We set goals to keep our vision alive and map our route. However, goals are not written in marble. Our goals may change. Sometimes people feel bad about changing their goals because they see it as lack of staying power. For others it is a response to new opportunities.

Change of direction

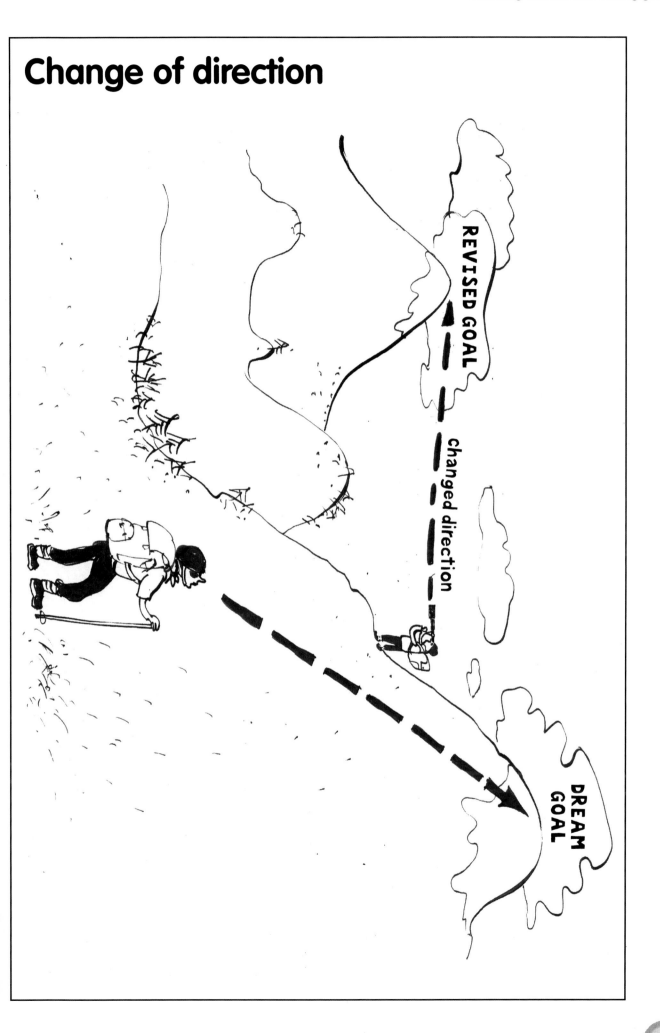

What makes a good life?

Many of us adults have never been asked to think:

– who we really are

– what we consider to be the most important aspect of our lives

– what it is that we want from life

– how we want to be remembered.

In some life-coaching courses people are asked to write their obituary. You could try this for yourself, should you feel it to be an interesting thing to do.

• Ask students to think of the most important aspects of their lives. You can ask them to come up with ideas and write them on the board for everyone to choose from.

• Accept all ideas, including the 'shocking' ones.

• Here are some prompts you may add to the list on the board; or you may show students the list below and ask them to select something from it.

1 Value my family.

2 Strive towards my goals.

3 Have enough money / be rich / appreciate who I am and what I have.

4 Keep an open mind.

5 Have a meaningful relationship.

6 Care about my friends.

7 Respect myself and show respect for others.

8 Enjoy the good things in life.

9 Learn self-control (eg anger, resentment).

10 Understand others and be tolerant.

11 Help people less fortunate than myself.

12 First take care of the important things in life (my *rocks*).

13 Keep learning new things.

14 Make a difference to someone else's life.

• When most students have chosen the key elements of their life, move to the creation of *mission statements*.

 This is a truly valuable activity, so if you think students are not taking on board the idea, you may need to return to it some other time.

What makes a good life?

My mission statement

My mission in life is to ....

....

....

....

....

....

....

....

Making learning relevant

In order to be effective we need to know why we do things.

WIIFM? (What's in it for me?)

There are things we just want to know and things we would like to be able to do.

We may want to know how a DVD recorder works, why people get depressed, how composers work or why yeast makes the dough rise.

We may want to be able to record a film on our new DVD recorder, to know how to help a depressed friend, to download a song we like or to make a birthday cake.

Most people want to know things when they need to know. Many people are *interested* to know why, how or when things happen.

If we have no need or interest, why would we bother to learn anything new?

Students need to know the reasons why they are expected to learn something or follow instructions.

What is your response when a student asks, 'Miss, why do I have to learn this?' or complains, 'I will never need to know this, Sir.'

Students have told me the responses they often hear:
'Because this is in the curriculum.'
'Because I say so!'
'Stop asking questions and get down to work.'

- Explain to students that knowing about things is in the head, while being able to do things is demonstrated by action. Often knowing and doing come together or follow each other, but not always. Give examples.

- Ask students to think of something they want to know and then of something they want to be able to do.

- Ask them how they learn when they want to know something.

- Talk about trial and error, following instructions, observing and copying, asking for help / explanation, surfing the net.

- Give out photocopied sheets and ask students to complete the sentences.

WIIFM? (What's in it for me?)

Think of something specific you would like to know and complete the sentences:

I want to know ....

I want to know this because ....

I will find out about this from ....

Think of something specific you would like to be able to do.

I would like to be able to ....

I want to do it because ....

I will learn to do it by ....

What's the use?
Learning outside school

'Relevant' can mean:

– useful now

– useful in the future (possibly)

– helpful

– practical

– connected with things / events / people in my life

– about something that matters to me

– interesting (I may not necessarily know why)

– enabling me to understand things I want to understand

– about me

– enjoyable.

What things are relevant to your life?

Is there anything you would be interested in learning because it is relevant to you?

- Explain what relevance is.

- Give a couple of examples of things relevant to you.

  – I watch *Dangerous Minds* or *Dead Poets Society* because I want to engage students.

  – I attend a marketing course because I want to start a business.

  – I read a book about stress because I suffer from bad migraines.

- Give out photocopied sheets and ask students to write what they have learnt *outside* school.

- Do not expect answers to all questions.

- Let students think about them and come back to the questions another time.

What's the use?
Learning outside school

What have you learnt *away from school* that you are glad you know?
Write in the boxes.

Useful straight away	Possibly useful in the future
Interesting	Helping me to understand things
About me	About other people

Useful or not useful? (1)

There are some people who learn just because they simply love learning new things. They are excited about exploring new territories and broadening their horizons.

However, most of us learn best when we know that what we are learning is going to be in some way useful to us. Usefulness is the motivation for learning just as necessity is the mother of invention.

• Ask students to think what they have already learnt outside school that they believe *will not be* useful to them in the future.

• Ask students to think what they have already learnt outside school that they believe *will be* useful to them in the future.

• Give out photocopied worksheets and tell them to fill in the blanks.

• Ask students one by one to read out what they have written and write their ideas on the board.

• Encourage students to copy the things they have not written yet which they agree will be useful to them.

Useful or not useful? (1)

What have you learnt that WILL NOT BE useful to you in the future?

– From parents ....

– From books ....

– From TV ....

– From friends ....

– Somewhere else ....

What have you learnt that WILL BE useful to you in the future?

– From parents ....

– From books ....

– From TV ....

– From friends ....

– Somewhere else ....

What's the use?
Learning at school

One of the criticisms students frequently express is that they feel a lot of their school work is never going to be useful to them. As a consequence they frequently feel bored at school.

With a curriculum that has to be followed and exams to prepare for, can we even attempt to make learning more relevant to our students? If so, how?

How can we show them that some things that may seem irrelevant, are in fact relevant to what they want to do?

Could students themselves provide some answers?

- Give out photocopied sheets and ask students to think what they have learnt *at school*.

- Tell students to imagine that they have two hats: the first one is a 'complaining' hat, the other an 'appreciating' hat.

- Ask them to put their 'complaining' hat on and do this activity in a negative state of mind.

- Get them to change their hats and go through the grid in their 'appreciating' hat and do the activity in a positive state of mind.

- Ask students to write their thoughts in the grid on the sheet.

- Focus on any positive answers you get and encourage students to discuss the possibility of seeing more of what they learn at school as relevant to them.

What's the use?
Learning at school

Your two hats

What have you learnt at school that is…

not useful now	useful now
not useful in the future	**possibly useful in the future**

Useful or not useful? (2)

There are some people who learn just because they simply love learning new things. They are excited about exploring new territories and broadening their horizons.

However, most of us learn best when we know that what we are learning is going to be in some way useful to us. Usefulness is the motivation for learning just as necessity is the mother of invention.

- Ask students what they have already learnt in the three core subjects that they think *will not be* useful to them in the future.

- Ask students what they have already learnt that they think *will be* useful to them in the future.

- Photocopy the worksheet and tell them to write their answers in the grid.

- Ask students one by one to read out what they have written and write their ideas on the board.

- Encourage students to copy the things they have not written yet which they agree will be useful to them.

Useful or not useful? (2)

In the boxes below write what useful and not useful things you have learnt in these lessons.

	Useful	Not useful
English		
Maths		
Science		

Relevance and the way we learn (1)

The purpose of this activity is to make students aware of the fact that people's learning needs vary. Bringing to students' attention the huge diversity of ways in which people learn can boost their sense of self-worth and show them the validity of varied learning strategies.

Teenage brains are 'work in progress'. Not all teenagers develop the capacity for abstract thought at the same time, which is why concrete, hands-on learning is still very much needed in secondary school. Failure to include kinaesthetic learning strategies in your lessons may result in many students' inability to see any relevance in what they learn and eventually lead to frustration and failure.

- Photocopy and give out the worksheet.

- Ask students to mark on the sheet everything that describes them best.

- Tell students to pair up and compare their answers.

- Encourage them to share their findings with two or three other students.

- Encourage students to notice the amazing diversity of ways in which people learn.

 If we don't teach students the way they learn, we are wasting their time and ours.

Relevance and the way we learn (1)

How do you remember things best?

When you want to remember something:

☐ Do you want to see it in writing?

☐ Do you like to look at a picture / a diagram / a graph?

☐ Do you like to watch a film / a video explaining it?

☐ Do you like to see it written in colour / printed on coloured paper?

☐ Do you like to doodle / walk about / swing in your chair / play with Blu-Tack®?

☐ Do you need to read and make notes at the same time?

☐ Do you like to swing on your chair / walk around while repeating it to yourself?

☐ Do you need to underline (in colour?), highlight, rewrite it a few times?

☐ Do you like to say it aloud to yourself?

☐ Do you like to explain it to somebody?

☐ Do you want someone to tell you about it?

☐ Do you like to play it on tape over and over again?

HOW CAN I REMEMBER THINGS BETTER?

What else do you do when you want to remember something?

Relevance and the way we learn (2)

Students frequently think that what they are supposed to learn has no relevance to their lives, their plans or their goals.

They need to be encouraged to reflect whether it is the subject itself or perhaps *the way* in which they are expected to learn that makes the learning seem meaningless.

- Photocopy and give out the worksheet.

- Ask students to mark on the sheet everything that describes them best.

- Tell students to pair up and compare their answers.

- Encourage them to share their findings with two or three other students.

- Encourage students to notice the amazing diversity of ways in which people learn.

 The important thing to remember is that people do their best thinking in very different circumstances.

Relevance and the way we learn (2)

How do you think best?

When you need to think, to solve a problem, to be creative:

☐ Do you need to be alone?

☐ Do you need to be with someone to 'think aloud'?

☐ Do you need silence?

☐ Do you need some 'background noise': music, TV, people talking in the next room?

☐ Do you like to be still, sit in a chair or lie on the sofa?

☐ Do you need to walk about, swing in a chair or hammock, manipulate objects like a pen, Blu-Tack® etc.?

☐ Does all the thinking happen in your head?

☐ Do you need to draw graphs, diagrams or pictures, or make mind maps to clarify things for yourself?

☐ Do you think best in the morning, almost the moment you wake up?

☐ Do you have your best ideas just before falling asleep at night?

The relevance chain

Very often we find it difficult, if not impossible, to help students see the relevance of what we are teaching them. Why? Because we ourselves don't have convincing answers!

This activity is an example of how you could attempt to show your students the way they could see the progression from immediate to long-term relevance.

- Read the examples from the bottom upwards.

- Give students the following instructions:

  – Think of something you are told to learn that in your opinion has no relevance to your life.

  – Write it in the bottom oval on the worksheet.

  – Write your life goal or some short-term goal at the top.

  – Now see if it is possible to find out whether what you have to learn may indeed have some connection with your goal.

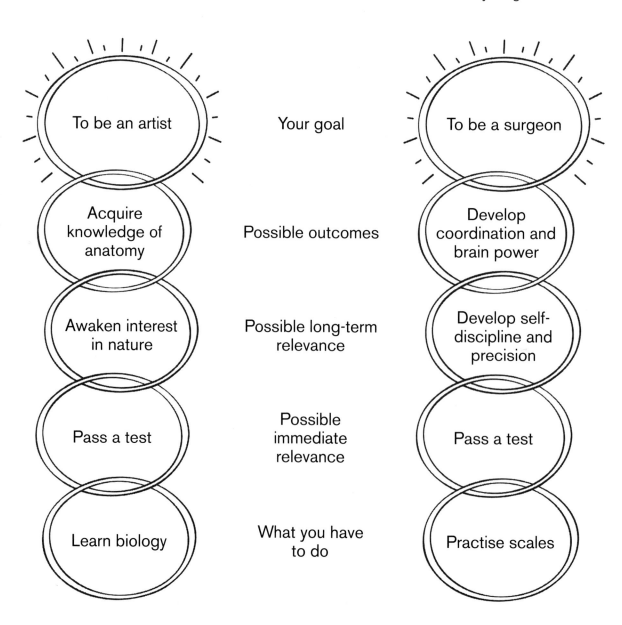

The relevance chain

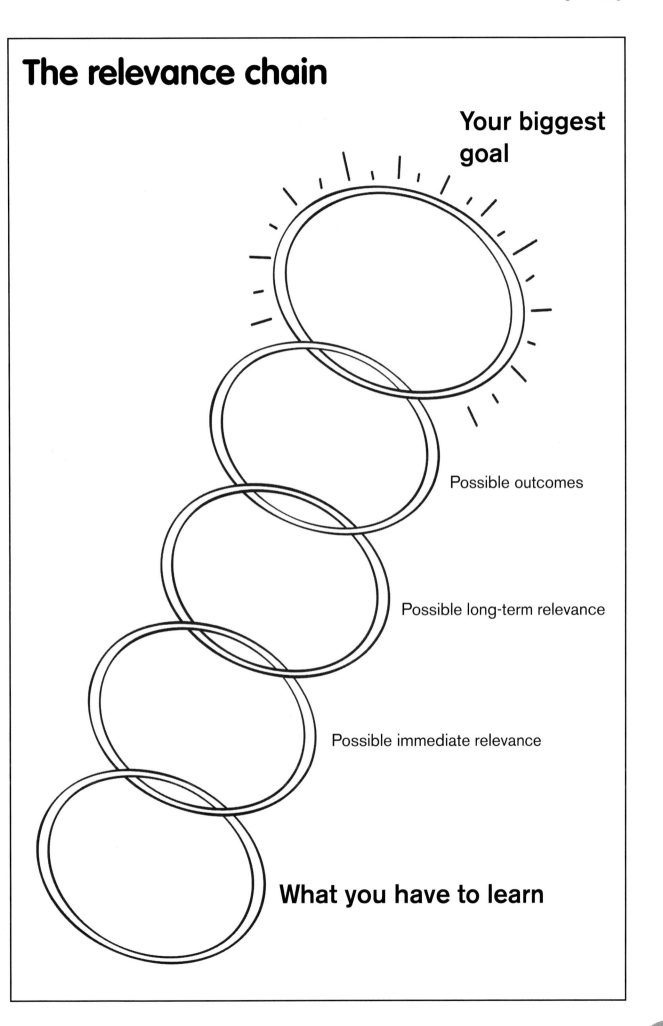

Your biggest goal

Possible outcomes

Possible long-term relevance

Possible immediate relevance

What you have to learn

What to say if you don't know what to say

Students sometimes complain that they can see no sense in learning certain things. It also happens that teachers themselves see little sense in introducing students to some of the topics recommended by the curriculum. While honesty is often the best way forward, sharing with students your doubts as to the relevance of the things they are learning will undoubtedly demotivate them even more.

Here is what you could do instead:

- Read the text overleaf to your students or let them read it to themselves.

- Ask students to think of similar scenarios and let them discuss their ideas in groups.

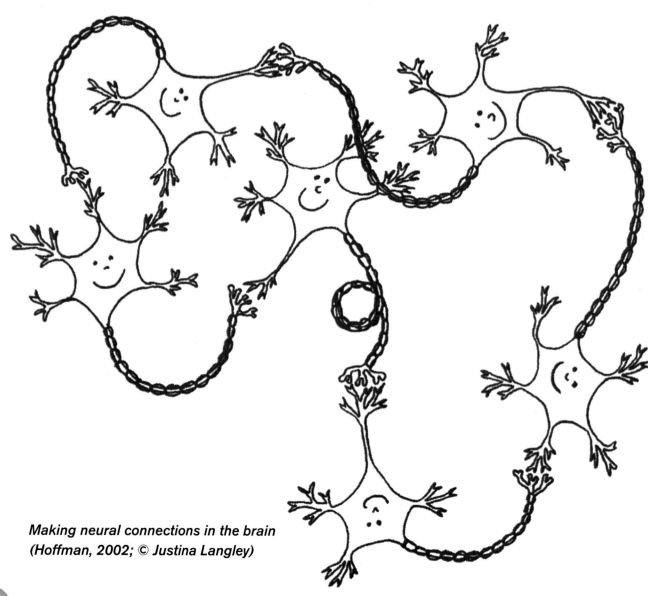

Making neural connections in the brain (Hoffman, 2002; © Justina Langley)

What to say if you don't know what to say

Use it or lose it

Have you ever watched footballers during their training sessions? When a team comes down to the pitch, they don't start playing football straight away. Instead, they do a lot of stretching, running, push-ups and bouncing the ball with their knees, elbows, shoulders, head and feet. Only after a while do they start playing football. Why is that? This is because all their muscles need to be strengthened and all joints have to be flexible. Without this initial training, without warming up, players could either do harm to their bodies or simply not be ready for action.

Your brain is a kind of muscle too. A muscle that needs to be stretched and exercised like all your other muscles if you want it to function efficiently. Everything you learn, no matter what it is, creates a neural connection in your brain. The more neural connections, the stronger and more efficient your thinking muscle!

So every time you have to learn something that is not interesting for you, think about what it does for your brain; it is making your brain stronger, more flexible and better equipped for learning things you will want to learn in future.

And this is why every single thing you learn is in some way relevant to your life!

If you don't exercise and stretch your brain in many directions, you will not be creating neural connections and your ability to think, learn, be creative will literally shrink!

Find the missing links

Finding a connection between the things we have to do and the things we want to achieve is often a big challenge.

It may seem impossible at times to find a connection, but if we take time to stop and think about it we may surprise ourselves with the results.

However, this kind of thinking requires practice and determination.

- Tell students to treat this activity as a puzzle.

- Ask them to find the 'missing links' between the thing that has to be done and the goal.

- Accept all responses no matter how impossible / silly / funny they are. In fact, encourage students to think 'outside the box' and have fun doing it.

Find the missing links

I have to...   **My goal is...**

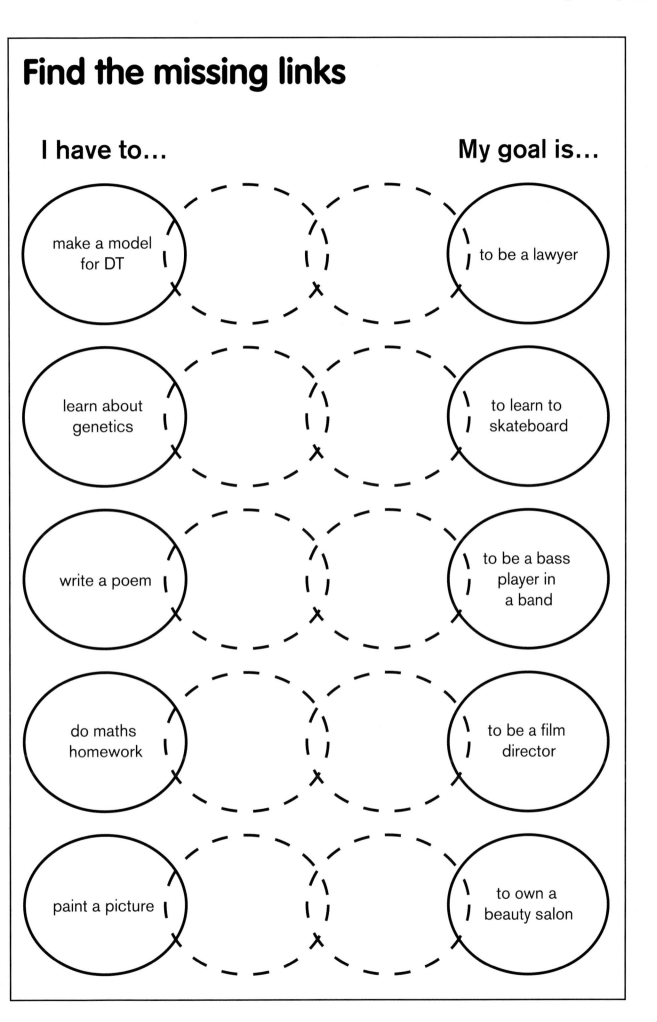

make a model for DT

learn about genetics

write a poem

do maths homework

paint a picture

to be a lawyer

to learn to skateboard

to be a bass player in a band

to be a film director

to own a beauty salon

Your relevance ladder

Working towards a goal almost always involves doing some things we don't particularly enjoy. It is not always easy to see how what we need to do is really connected with our big *goal*. What may help is attempting to find out how one step can lead to another so that eventually the seemingly unconnected mini-goals will form a continuum bringing us to the desired goal.

- Ask students to write a couple of goals they may have.

- Ask them to think of a few things they are expected to study for a test or an exam.

- Tell them to write their goal at the top of the ladder and the thing they need to study at the bottom.

- Suggest they find the outcome of each step they take.

- You may want to read them the example here to clarify what you expect them to do.

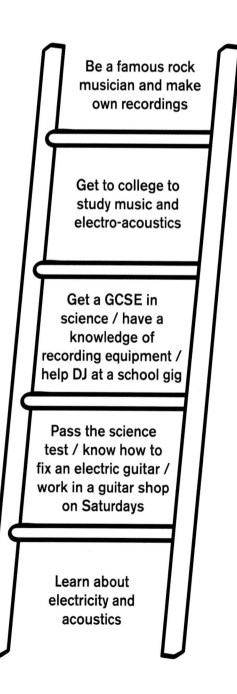

Be a famous rock musician and make own recordings

Get to college to study music and electro-acoustics

Get a GCSE in science / have a knowledge of recording equipment / help DJ at a school gig

Pass the science test / know how to fix an electric guitar / work in a guitar shop on Saturdays

Learn about electricity and acoustics

Your relevance ladder

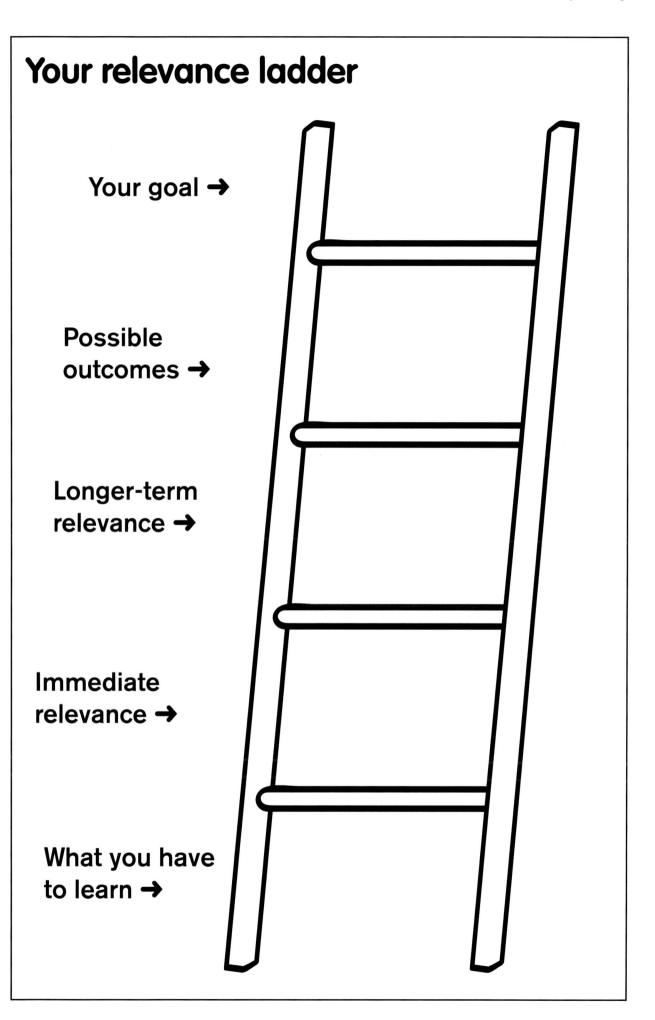

Your goal →

Possible
outcomes →

Longer-term
relevance →

Immediate
relevance →

What you have
to learn →

Raising confidence

Believing in yourself and your ability to learn is your master key to success.

Your achievements great and small

It's good to remind ourselves about the great number of things we have learnt in our lives. Frequently, we either take our skills and knowledge for granted or we forget that there was a time when we didn't have particular knowledge or a particular skill.

Reminding ourselves about things we have learnt and achieved can help us feel more confident and help us believe in our ability to learn.

- Remind students they have already learnt a tremendous number of things.

- Ask them to think what it is they can do now that they couldn't do or didn't know when they were younger.

- Write their ideas on the board.

- Give students a copy of the worksheet and encourage them to fill all the lines with their achievements so far.

- When everybody has filled a number of blanks ask them to share with others what they have written.

Nobody can do everything but everybody can do something.
Jack Canfield

Your achievements great and small

Think about the things you know and can do now that you could not do when you were a child.

When you run out of ideas, see what other people have written and put it on your list if something is also true about you.

1	16
2	17
3	18
4	19
5	20
6	21
7	22
8	23
9	24
10	25
11	26
12	27
13	28
14	29
15	30

Your many intelligences: appreciate your strengths

Working with multiple intelligences is one of the best, most effective ways to boost students' confidence and general sense of self-worth.

Over 30 years ago Howard Gardner shattered the fixed IQ myth. Using the research findings of a number of scientists and psychologists he suggested that each person has a number of different intelligences, each of which may be developed if the appropriate stimuli are applied (Gardner, 1985).

What a wonderful and immediate self-image booster, and what great prospects for every single learner!

We are all intelligent.

We are intelligent in a different way.

We may, if we work on it, develop our intelligences.

For more ideas on how to help students discover their strengths, see *Introducing Children to Their Intelligences* by Eva Hoffman (2001)

- Give each student a copy of the 'Intelligences mind map'. Tell them that each arm of the map represents one intelligence, one kind of strength.

- Say to students:

  – Every human being is intelligent; every one is intelligent in a different way.

  – Some of your intelligences are probably better developed than others.

  – Your well-developed intelligences are your strengths, the things you are good at, the things you like doing.

  – You can develop your intelligences if you work to improve them.

- Discuss each branch of the mind map and talk with students about people they know who are strong in a particular intelligence. Tell them to write these people's names on the lines.

- Ask students to think which is their strongest intelligence and to mark it with their favourite colour.

- Encourage students to mark one or two other strong intelligences they have.

- Have students share their mind maps with partners. You may also encourage them to find people who are either very similar or very different from themselves.

Your many intelligences: appreciate your strengths

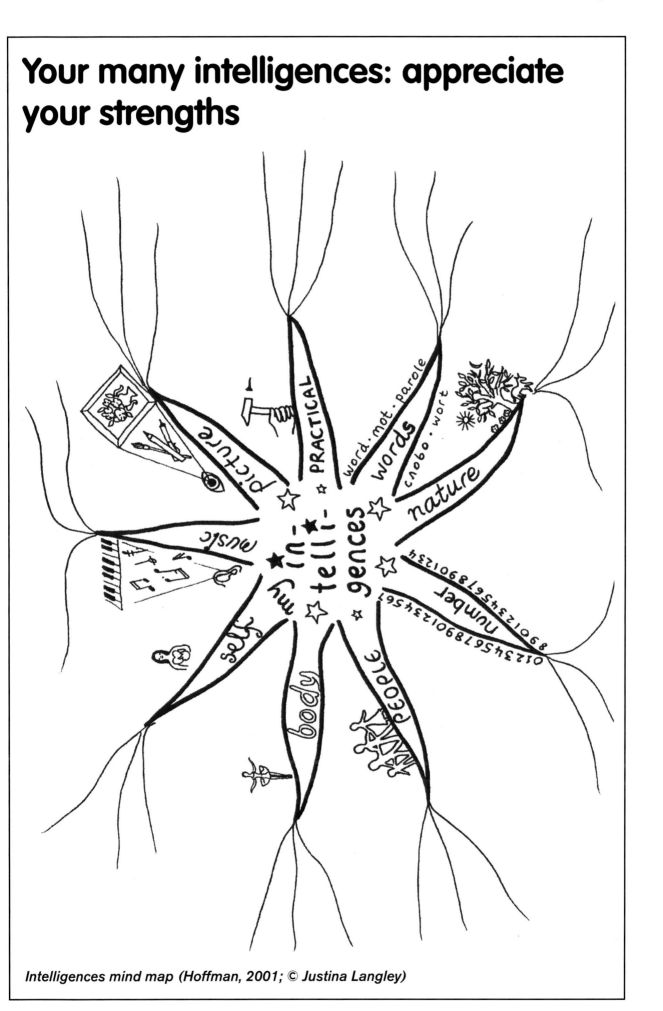

Intelligences mind map (Hoffman, 2001; © Justina Langley)

Watch your tongue! (1)

This activity is suitable for younger students. Saying 'I can't' over and over again makes us feel weak, helpless and useless.

Many young people say 'I can't' before they've even attempted doing whatever they are supposed to do. Young people are often told not to use the phrase, but what are they supposed to say if they think they *can't*?!

- Tell students about the danger of using unhelpful words: when you say things often enough, your brain will believe they are right. Saying 'I can't' stops the brain from thinking, remembering and learning in general.

- Tell students that from now on nobody is allowed to say 'I can't'; instead, if they face a challenge they have to choose one of the following:

  – 'I need more time'

  – 'I need to practise'

  – 'I need help'.

- Give each student two copies of the picture and tell them to colour one in. Tell them to cross out the 'I can't' bottom image, to make it dark and horrible. Encourage them to use attractive colours for the three balloons.

- The first copy will be glued in their journal, the other one can be taken home to show parents what the student is learning and to explain why using the right language is important.

If you think you can, or if you think you can't, you're right.
Henry Ford

Watch your tongue! (1)

Show you care

Students don't care how much you know until they know how much you care.

- Ask students what helps them feel more confident.

- Tell them to write their ideas on sticky labels and display them for everyone to see.

- Give out the photocopied sheets and ask students to pick from the list:

  - what they're already experiencing at school

  - something they would like to experience more of.

- Ask students what they think *they* could do to receive the treatment that could boost their confidence.

Show you care

What would help you feel more confident?

Look at the list, add your own ideas if you wish and then tick the three most important things.

I would like my teachers…

☐ to be friendly and smile more often

☐ to encourage me

☐ to believe I can do better

☐ to listen to my opinions

☐ to praise me (for trying too!)

☐

☐

Mind–body: the talking mirror

The way we see ourselves is crucial for our self-confidence. The trouble is that our perception of ourselves is often inaccurate or at best incomplete.

This incomplete, inaccurate perception of ourselves is likely to have a damaging effect on our confidence.

If we see ourselves as unattractive, not bright enough, not clever enough, how can we possibly succeed? How will others perceive us?

If we see ourselves as attractive enough, bright enough, clever enough, what are our chances of succeeding? How will others perceive us?

- Demonstrate the activity by adopting the two extreme body postures yourself.

- Tell students to practise the postures with partners.

- Recommend that students have their photographs taken. Seeing themselves in those contrasting images will be much more effective than talking about it.

- Have them glue the two pictures in their journal (or on their mirror at home).

- Discuss with students the effect body posture has on the mind.

Mind–body: the talking mirror

Stand in front of a mirror and practise looking positive, happy and confident. When you look convincing enough, ask a friend to take a photo of you and glue it in the frame.

Now stand in front of a mirror and practise looking negative, miserable and painfully shy. When ready, have your picture taken.

Does your body language show what you feel?
Can your body language change the way you feel?
Write your thoughts in your journal.

Mind–body: from slump to pump

Our mind and body are connected and interdependent: how we use our body will affect the thoughts we think and whatever we think will affect our body.

Even a simple change in body posture can significantly change our confidence and the way we see the world.

- Tell students to slump in their chairs, hang their heads down, shoulders bent, and sigh.

- Let them stay in this position for a moment.

- Ask them to become aware of how they feel when their bodies assume this posture.

- Now tell them to take a deep breath and stretch their arms up high to the ceiling.

- Tell them to sit up, head high, back straight, and let them stay in this posture for a while.

- Ask students how they feel now that their body posture has changed.

- Now add a smile and see what effect this has.

Mind–body: from slump to pump

When you make a simple change to the way you sit or stand, you are sending a message to your brain how 'it is supposed to feel'.

You are also telling the people around you whether or not you ARE a naturally confident person.

Mind—body: light and energy

Aikido is one of the martial arts. Aikido masters teach that when we put our attention in the very centre of our body we become truly strong, both psychologically and physically.

- Give pupils the following instructions:

  – Stand up straight, take a deep breath in… and breathe out.

  – Place your hand over your stomach and find a point two centimetres below your navel.

  – Imagine a sphere of light and energy in this spot and 'move' it towards the centre of your body, half-way between your spine and the point below your navel.

  – You have now found the place where your life force is stored.

  – Visualise breathing through this spot.

- Give out the photocopied sheet with the body shape and ask pupils to mark the energy centre.

- Tell them to write the words 'strength', 'confidence', 'peace', 'energy' all around the figure.

 Whenever we feel nervous, weak, upset, we can feel our energy centre and use the energy to change this feeling into a sensation of peaceful strength!

Mind–body: light and energy

Mark the spot of your energy centre.
Always remember that it's there.

MOTIVATING THE TEENAGE MIND

Teacher's
page

Mind–body: feeling confident

Tell, show and practise the following with your students.

Here is how you can feel more confident:

1 Stand up, straighten your back, look ahead and breathe. Visualise breathing through the part of your body which is sensitive to the way you feel; for many people it is their stomach area (solar plexus), but it could be any other part of the body.

2 Imagine you are zipping up your fleece and move your hand all the way from below your navel up to your lower lip. Do it twice. If you are in a public place and don't want to make a spectacle of yourself, just imagine zipping up; it will work too.

3 Stand in a 'warrior' posture and breathe, feeling strong and confident.

Mind–body: feeling confident

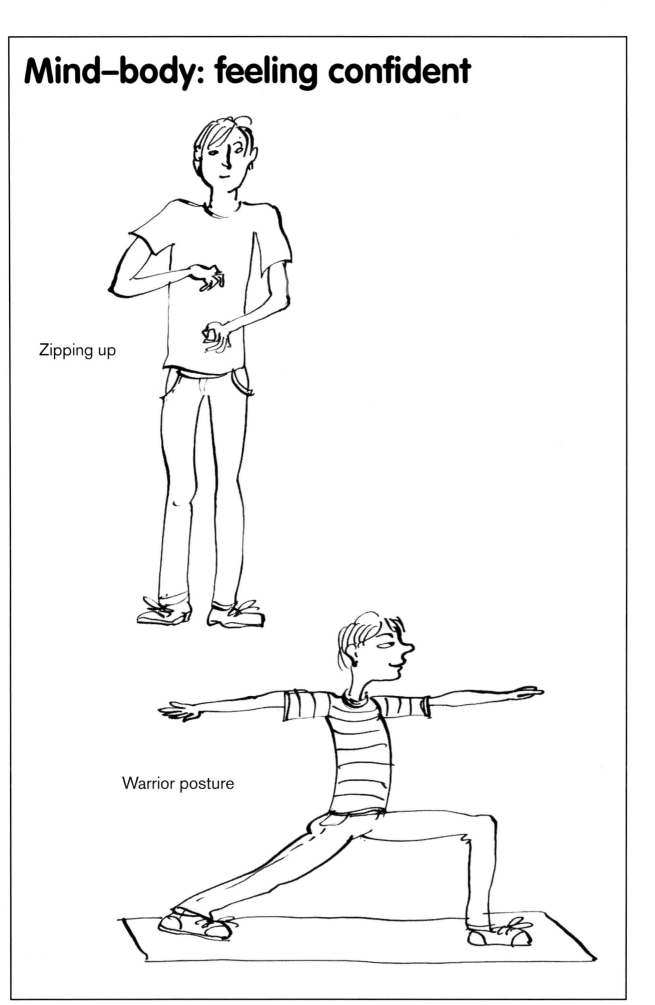

Zipping up

Warrior posture

Belonging

**Knowing that we are a part of a group helps
us feel safer, stronger and protected.**

**For most young people a sense of belonging
to a group is essential in developing their
confidence.**

**Students who feel they are outsiders
often become withdrawn and insecure.
Consequently, they will look for the sense of
belonging elsewhere. It's fine if it is a club or
some kind of interest group; not so good if it
is a gang.**

- Ask students what makes them feel they
  belong to the school community:

  – their tutor group, a band, an orchestra, a
    choir, after-school clubs, the school council,
    trips, charity walks.

- Identify students who are withdrawn, who
  separate themselves from the group or are
  excluded by the group. It is the 'invisible' ones
  who need your attention and possibly help.
  But don't rush to conclusions as they may
  have strong ties with their families or some out
  of school interest group.

Discussion points

– Why do people want to *belong* to a group?

– Why do some people feel they don't belong?

– What can the feeling of isolation lead to?

Belonging

In the six 'petals' write the names of some of the groups you belong to.

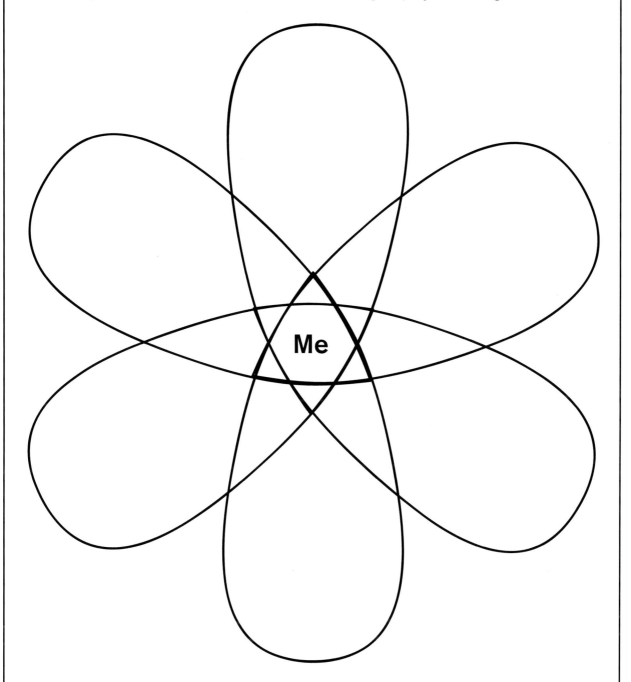

Some groups you may like to consider:
* your family • your extended family • a friendship group • an interest group
* a 'hanging out' group • clubs • teams • a band • a choir • your class
* your tutor group • your school • a community • your race • a church
* a political party • a nation • humankind • other

Can do, can't do

People's actions reflect their beliefs.
They tend to act in certain ways in order
to prove that what they believe is right.

If we are not happy with our lives, we need
to change our beliefs. Alternatively, we can
start by changing the way we do things.
This will eventually reform our unhelpful
beliefs.

PUT ALL
YOUR
LIMITING
BELIEFS
HERE

- Bring a rubbish bin to class and write on its
  side in big letters:
  'Put your negative beliefs about yourself –
  here!'

- Ask students to write on sticky labels any
  negative beliefs they hold about themselves.
  Then tell them to tear the notes into small
  pieces and throw them into the bin.

- Ask students to think how people act when
  they believe they cannot do things. Write their
  ideas on a flip-chart.

- Ask how people act when they believe they
  can do things. Write students' ideas on
  another flip-chart.

- Give out photocopied sheets and ask students
  to write the eight points where they belong in
  the circle.

- Discuss with students how they might set
  about becoming a *can do* person.

 **Your thoughts affect your actions.
Your actions affect your thoughts.**

Can do, can't do

Write the eight points (or the numbers) where you think they belong in the circle.

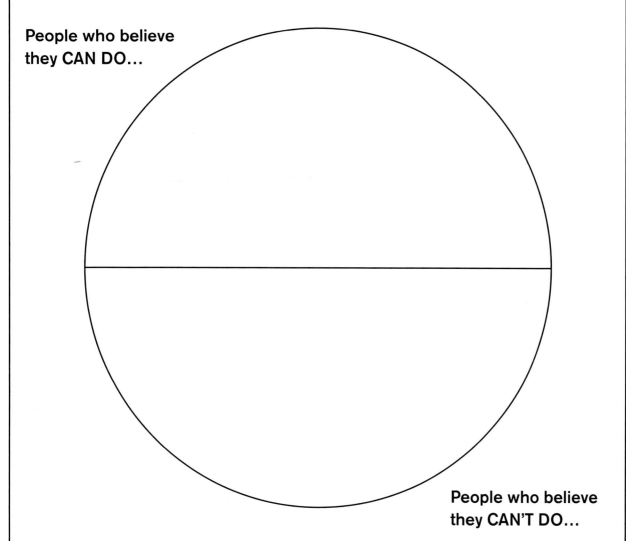

**People who believe
they CAN DO…**

**People who believe
they CAN'T DO…**

1 …take no action

2 …get into the 'driving seat' of life

3 …think about solutions and possibilities

4 …drift wherever situations take them

5 …make things happen

6 …wait for something to happen

7 …get things done

8 …see only problems, barriers and obstacles

Crystal ball predictions

Many successful people have done well at school. There are also many who did not perform well at school and yet have done extremely well in life. Apart from the famous people whose names we often quote to support this statement such as Albert Einstein, Thomas Edison, F. W. Woolworth, Winston Churchill, Walt Disney, Fred Astaire, Richard Branson and very many others, there have been thousands, millions probably, who have barely survived school and yet have lived successful and fulfilled lives.

We educators frequently make the mistake of trying to play god: we predict exam results, we even predict students' futures. This can be harmful because predictions often become self-fulfilling prophecies. We risk clipping students' wings before they even attempt to fly!

Let's acknowledge that every human being has huge potential. It is our duty as educators to help our students become aware of the range of possibilities within them.

We, on the other hand, need to be aware of the fact that we simply don't know what their potential really is, nor how and when it will manifest itself.

Time for reflection

Believe in all your students – not just the ones who do well and have a positive attitude to life and work.

Most importantly, learn to believe in those who are not great school achievers, those who are your cause for concern, those you don't particularly like.

These are the people who need you the most. They need you to believe in their ability to succeed in whatever they choose to do.

- Give out photocopied sheets and let students read the quotes.

- Ensure that everybody understands the fallibility of predictions.

- Ask students to write their conclusions in the box or on sticky labels,

  or

- ask everyone to read their conclusions out loud.

Crystal ball predictions

Here are a few opinions expressed by people in authority, people holding important positions, people who were knowledgeable and were considered authorities in their fields:

'There is no reason for any individual to have a computer in their home'
K. Olsen, President and Founder of Digital Equipment Corporation (1977)

'Airplanes are interesting toys but of no military value'
F. Foch, French military strategist (1911)

'Man will never reach the moon'
Dr L. Forest, inventor (1967)

'Television won't be able to hold on to any market it captures after the first six months'
D. Zanuck, Head of 20th Century-Fox (1946)

'For the majority of people tobacco has a beneficial effect'
Dr Ian Macdonald, surgeon (1967)

'The telephone cannot be seriously considered as a means of communication'
Western Union memo (1876)

'Everything that can be invented has been invented'
C. Duell, US Commissioner of patents (1899)

What conclusions can you draw from all this?
Write your thoughts in the box below.

143

Crystal balls at school

The education system expects students to comply and those who are born rebels hardly ever flourish within its constraints.

Just one person who unconditionally believes in another can dramatically influence their life. Let it be you!

The people listed on the next page did extremely well despite all the negative predictions. However, there is no way of knowing how many people have been damaged because they believed what teachers and parents thought about them.

- Read the text and decide whether this is what you want your students to know.

- Ask your students:

  – Has anybody ever told you that you are not good at something you wanted to do and that you have no chance of succeeding?

  – Did you believe them? Did you lose heart? Did you give up?

  – Have you considered the possibility that even people who you think should know better, may be terribly wrong?

- Discuss with students alternatives to formal education and the consequences of each choice:

  – home education

  – street education.

- Show that choosing to opt out of formal education and making it in the world may require true passion, dedication, self-motivation and a good dose of resilience.

It's worth remembering that people are positively influenced by those who believe in them.

Crystal balls at school

Did you know ...?

- Winston Churchill, Britain's Prime Minister during WW2, did poorly at school and before he became prime minister his life was full of defeats and setbacks.

- Richard Branson, a multi-millionaire entrepreneur and the creator of the Virgin Group, disliked school and was a poor student.

- Thomas Edison, a genius and brilliant inventor who made a great number of discoveries, was pronounced 'unteachable' – his teachers said he was too stupid to learn anything.

- Albert Einstein's school report described him as mentally slow, unsociable and 'adrift forever in his foolish dreams'. Einstein went on to become the most prominent scientist of the 20th century.

- Ludwig van Beethoven, one of the most famous German composers, was considered by his music teacher to be a hopeless student.

These are just a few names from a long list of people who failed to succeed in formal education and yet became famous and extremely successful.

 This does not mean that the condition for being famous is failing at school! It means that it is possible that some people who do not do well in the school environment blossom later in life due to their passion, hard work and talent. Those talents have either not been recognised at school or may have developed later in life.

Watch your tongue! (2)

Negative generalisations and unqualified statements have the power to push us deep into negativity, sometimes even into depression.

Just reading statements like the ones in the activity can make us feel lousy! They are all generalisations of particular incidents that triggered negative feelings in the speaker. Although deep down in our hearts we probably *do* know they are not true, our brains, which in this case show no sense of humour, take them seriously.

The trick is to bring back the details and become more specific in our statements.

When we become specific in the way we express our feelings, we will not only get closer to the truth but the negativity will not drag us down.

- Explain to students what a generalisation is.

- Think of a negative generalisation you say or think about yourself.

- Tell students what you say about yourself, eg:
  - 'I always lose my keys.'

- Explain to students that every time you repeat the statement a neural pattern in your brain gets stronger and stronger. Eventually the statement becomes a self-fulfilling prophecy.

- Show students how to change generalisations into statements that better reflect the reality and therefore become less dramatic and less negative.

Here is how you can make general statements more specific.

Instead of saying,   'Nobody appreciates what I do'
say something like,   'My brother didn't appreciate my help last night.'

Instead of saying,   'People are horrible to me'
say something like,   'Brian and Sam call me names.'

Watch your tongue! (2)

Do you ever say things like...?

Nobody appreciates what I do.
I can never remember people's names.
I am rubbish at art.
Everyone criticises me.
I hate winter.
I can't do maths.
People are horrible to me.

In the grid write four sweeping generalisations you make about yourself.
Reconstruct the statements, making them as specific as you can.

When reconstructing your statements, answer simple questions: who did what,
when and where.

General	Specific
I can never...	
Nobody ever...	
I always...	
Everybody thinks that I...	

Watch your tongue! (3)

When we use 'victim language' we turn ourselves into victims. We give away control over our thoughts, our mood, our actions.

'Victims' tend to:

– blame others

– moan, groan and complain about just anything

– be passive and wait for 'things' to happen in their lives

– be very easily offended

– spit out venom in anger (only to regret it later).

If you ever say,
'I can't help it, that's the way I am',

you are implying:
I was born like this; it's my genes, my upbringing, my situation and my life that made me the way I am. I don't have the ability to change and that is why I am not responsible for what I say, or for the way I act.

If you ever say,
'If my boss / partner / boy / girlfriend wasn't so hopeless everything would be fine',

you are implying:
My boss / partner / boy / girlfriend is the cause of all my problems. Nothing to do with me.

• Talk to students about victim language.

• Give out copies of the activity sheet and ask your students to complete the sentences.

• Remind them that they will not have to share their thoughts with anyone.

Watch your tongue! (3)

'Poor me' or 'I am in charge'

Complete the sentences.

When I get into 'poor me' mode...

⚡ I tend to blame ....

☀ Instead, I could ....

⚡ I often complain about ....

☀ Instead, I could ....

⚡ I do nothing about my problem and wait for ....

☀ Instead, I could ....

⚡ I get easily offended when ....

☀ Instead, I could ....

⚡ I say angry / hurtful / rude words ....

☀ Instead, I could ....

How to damage your confidence

Treat the activity as a game; this reverse psychology activity shows the folly of what we do to ourselves and helps identify what we might do instead.

Although it is often others who trigger our feelings of insecurity and low self-esteem, most frequently it is our own thoughts that do us the most harm.

The way we see ourselves and the thoughts we think about ourselves are the all-important determinants of how we feel and how we behave in consequence.

- Ask students to share their ideas of how they think people ruin their self-confidence and write them in the bricks.

- Acknowledge every suggestion positively.

- Help students discriminate between what other people do to us and what we do to ourselves.

- Read out the following list and ask students to see whether they have included any of these 'confidence destroyers'.

  I might:

  – see myself as a victim / loser

  – blame others and the world for everything bad that happens in my life

  – not notice or remember my achievements

  – compare myself with others who are 'better'

  – take to heart every negative comment made about me

  – nurture a firm belief that I can't do what others can

  – refuse to give things a go in case I fail

  – disbelieve any positive comments made about me

  – use generalisations such as:
    I can *never* get things right
    I *always* mess up
    Nobody trusts me to do anything
    Everybody thinks I am dumb.

- Encourage students to identify something they can do differently.

How to damage your confidence

Imagine that your goal is to destroy your self-confidence.
How will you go about it?

Fill the bricks with your destructive thoughts and actions.

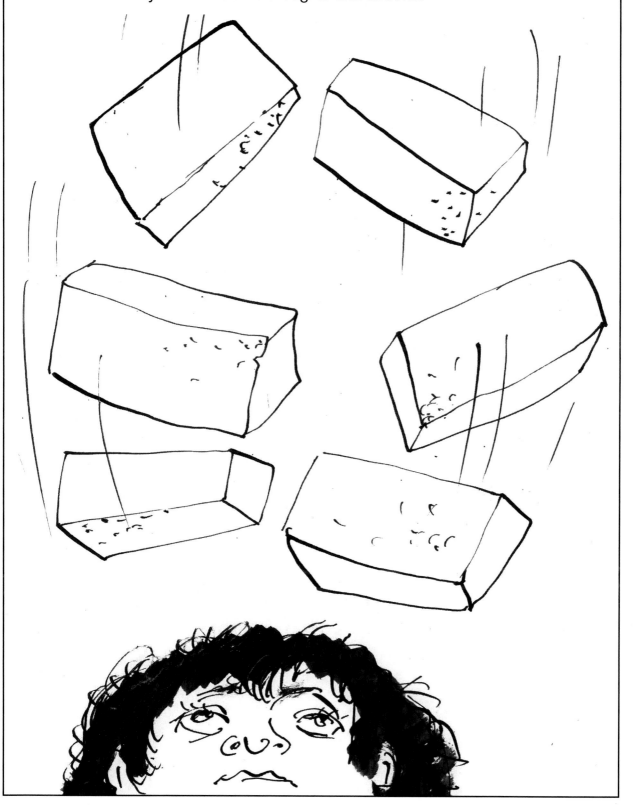

Be in control

We feel what we feel.

**We may not always find it easy to change how
we feel but we can choose the way we act.**

**Being able to control the way we act gives us
a sense of power, strength and confidence, as
we realise we do not need to be at the mercy
of our emotions.**

- Ask students what they do when they
  get angry.

- Have students come up with answers?
  If necessary, give the following prompts:

  – use foul language

  – cry

  – find a quiet place and contemplate

  – smash things

  – hit your opponent

  – say things you often regret later

  – walk away feeling hurt, offended and
    helpless

  – harm yourself

  – yell.

- Tell students all these responses cause
  harmful stress and are a waste of energy.

- Say to students:

  Here is what you can do when you get angry.

  With the thumb of your right hand press the
  middle of your left palm and make tiny circular
  anticlockwise movements. This is your pause
  button.

  Now imagine a time when you were angry and
  repeat this movement, thinking to yourself
  'This is how I stay calm'.

Be in control

When you are angry, frustrated and feel like lashing out, here is what you can do.

| Take a deep breath in and slowly breathe out | Press your 'pause button' and hold it for a moment | Confidently say what you think and how you feel |

Remember
You feel what you feel
but you CAN control your behaviour.

Remember
You can only control yourself,
never other people (alas!).

Remember
When your index finger points at someone else,
three other fingers point at ... YOU!

Remember
Breathe and press your 'pause button' whenever you get angry!

Five per cent more confidence

Nathaniel Branden, often considered the father of the self-esteem movement, uses sentence completion activities in his books and counselling workshops (Branden, 1997).

This activity is an example of how the idea of sentence completion can be adapted for a specific purpose and a specific audience.

Never confuse confidence with arrogance.
Those who put others down, who use bullying tactics to get what they want, most frequently have poor self-esteem and lack real confidence.

- Encourage students to complete each sentence on the worksheet, writing the first thing that comes to mind.

- Ask them to complete the sentences once more, this time changing 5 per cent to 50 per cent more confidence.

- Ask students to compare their second responses with their previous ones and see whether they notice any significant difference.

NB It often happens that the responses, whatever the percentage, are very similar. Discuss the possible reasons for the similarity.

A shift in the way they think is what really matters.

Share with students and discuss this six-question activity:

1 How many minutes are there in a day? (1,440)

2 How many thoughts do you think a day? (between 12,000 and 65,000)

3 How many of your thoughts are the same every day? (about 70 per cent)

4 How many of them do you think destroy your confidence?

5 How many of them help you feel confident and good about yourself?

6 How many of the 1,440 minutes a day are you prepared to devote to improving your confidence?

Five per cent more confidence

If I had five per cent more confidence when I talk to adults,

I would ....

If I had five per cent more confidence in my ability to succeed,

I would ....

If I had five per cent more confidence when I meet new people,

I would ....

If I had five per cent more confidence in a new situation,

I would ....

Next time you find yourself in the situations described above, see yourself as five per cent more confident and act accordingly!

Who you are makes a difference

Each of us is different from all other people; the combination of our genetic code, our life experiences and our 'brain wiring' is absolutely unique. There is nobody in the whole world exactly like us. This makes us special and the same is true for everybody!

Our special uniqueness means we can all learn from everyone we encounter and we can share our insights with others to enrich their lives.

- Hand out photocopied sheets or individual quotes

  or

- play some relaxing music and read the quotations to your students.

- Alternatively, put them on PowerPoint with background music and let students read them for themselves.

- Ask students to pick a quote they particularly like and talk with a partner, explaining why the quote resonates with them.

- At the end of the session go through all the quotes once more – a PowerPoint slide show is ideal for reviews.

- If you decide to give students the whole sheet, ask them to find their best quote and glue it in their journal.

Who you are makes a difference

Find the quote you like best, cut it out and glue it in your journal.

Nobody can do everything but everybody can do something. Find out what it is you can do and give it all you have. This is your road to success. *Jack Canfield, 2001*	We are what we think. With our thoughts we make the world. *The Buddha*
If you focus on your weaknesses, you strengthen them. If you focus on your strengths, they will get even stronger. Be careful what you focus on.	It is important to bear in mind that academic success in school is not necessarily a reliable indicator of how a person will succeed in life.
Even one person who truly believes in you can dramatically affect your life. It could be you!	Learn from your mistakes but always remember your successes and get your strength from them.
Treat your failures as challenges and use them to find better ways of doing things.	When you believe you can, you are right. When you believe you can't, you are right too! *Henry Ford*

You become what you practise

'We are what we repeatedly do'
Aristotle

Nikki frequently says that she is shy and lacks confidence. When someone tells her that she seems to act confidently in many situations, she very confidently states that she definitely lacks confidence and that she is shy, extremely shy!

Is this really lack of confidence? It doesn't look like it. The problem is that Nikki is confident about the wrong thing: she is confident about the idea that she lacks confidence. The important thing is that every time Nikki says she lacks confidence, she creates a stronger and stronger pattern in her brain, turning her words into 'the truth'.

- Buy several pairs of large glasses (shops with party accessories sell them).

- On some write 'I am shy', on others 'I am confident'.

- Ask a volunteer to put on the 'I'm shy' glasses and to act in the way a shy person would. Then have them change the glasses and look at the world with confident eyes, acting in the way a confident person does.

- Talk to students about the choice they have: they can look at the world with their 'shy eyes' or their 'confident eyes'.

- Encourage them to make a poster / reminder with the words 'You become what you practise'.

You become what you practise

If you believe you are shy, you will be looking at the world with the eyes of a shy person. Your belief will make you shy.

If you believe you are confident, you will see the world around you with the eyes of a confident person. Your belief will make you more confident.

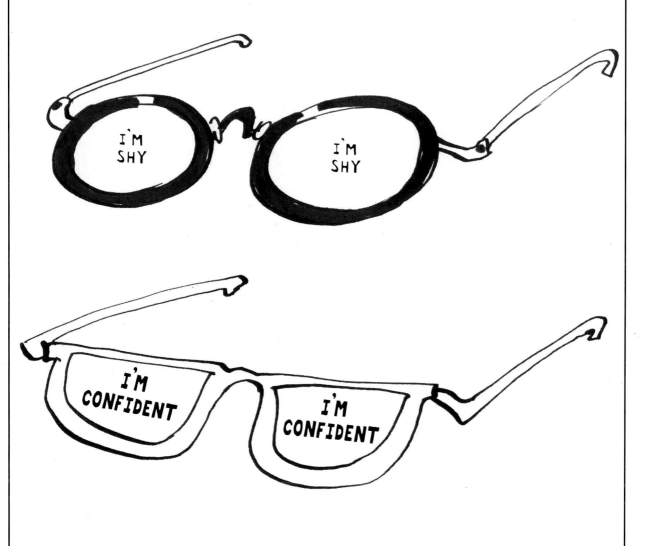

YOU BECOME WHAT YOU PRACTISE

Self-sabotage

Psychological studies by Albert Bandura show that people's beliefs about themselves and about how capable they are, can be an accurate predictor of their performance and future success (Bandura, 1977). Psychologists have called this 'a self-fulfilling prophecy'.

A negative self-fulfilling prophecy can ruin our confidence and with it our chances for success. A positive one can help build up confidence.

Human beings are truly good at self-sabotaging; we do things and think thoughts which destroy our confidence and our ability to succeed.

As Jack Canfield says, every time you think negative thoughts about your chances of success, it is as if you were trying to drive a car with your foot on the accelerator and the handbrake on (Canfield, 2001)!

- Explain to students the meaning of a self-fulfilling prophecy.

- Ask them if they have had negative thoughts about themselves that have eventually become reality.

- Tell them how negative self-fulfilling prophecies are ways of self-sabotaging.

- Ask them to think of other ways to represent self-sabotaging in pictorial form or in writing and record it in their journal.

Self-sabotage

Are you your best friend or your worst enemy?

Imagine the following:

You are going to a party and you would like to look good but for some strange reason at the last minute you put on your most unattractive clothes.

You are dying to see a film with your friends but when they invite you, you act as if you can't be bothered to go with them.

You would like to do well in the test but since you reckon you probably won't, you decide not to revise.

Does anybody you know ever do anything like that?
Write your examples of self-sabotage here.

Strengthening resilience

*Failing is often a temporary setback –
giving up is what makes it permanent.*

Learn a new skill

While in order to succeed it is necessary to think positively, it is also necessary to know that at times we will get things wrong, that at times we *will* fail. It often takes very many attempts to get things right. Every accomplished artist, dancer, scientist, writer, engineer, cook, musician or any other professional will confirm this.

It is essential to be able to deal with failure in a way which will help us learn from it rather than make us totally miserable.

- Plan to conduct the session outside the building or in the hall.

- Bring a few sets of juggling balls to the group.

- Ask students what is likely to happen with the balls when they start to learn juggling.

- Invite volunteers who have never done this before to come forward and try to juggle.

- Tell students that some people are naturally more ready to persevere than others but that everyone can choose to respond to a challenge in a more helpful way.

- Encourage students to act out different responses and see the funny side of some of them.

Learn a new skill

☐ I gave up almost immediately.

☐ I got impatient after trying a few times.

☐ I pretty quickly got angry that I couldn't do it, threw the balls in the corner and walked away.

☐ I tried and tried but gave up when it wasn't working.

☐ I tried and tried and then tried some more until I could do it!

What kept you going for as long as you did?

Persevere or give up?

When faced with a challenging task, all of us at some point experience the temptation to give up.

The difference between people is that some consistently give up while others tend to persevere against all odds.

- Ask students to think of something they tried doing but gave up when it proved difficult.

- Ask them to think of something they wanted to do and tried, tried and tried until they finally succeeded.

- Encourage them to share their stories with partners or with the whole group.

- Read aloud the story about two frogs.

- Ask them to illustrate the story or write a different one about the 'power of sticking with it'.

Persevere or give up?

Two frogs and a bucket of cream

One day two frogs were hopping happily along (as frogs do!) when all of a sudden they fell into a bucket. The bucket was filled with some strange white liquid the frogs had never seen or tasted before. They tried to jump out of the bucket but that was out of the question! The frogs quickly realised they were stuck! They tried thrashing around but the liquid only seemed to be getting thicker … It was becoming more and more difficult to move their legs! How scary was that?! Both frogs were getting tired and finally one of them said: 'I can't do it any more. I'm giving up!' and he slowly sank into the liquid and drowned.

The other frog was very tempted to resign himself to his fate but then decided to give it just one more go. With all the energy he had left he began thrashing around harder and harder until … he felt something solid under his feet! This 'something' was hard enough to allow him to stand on it and eventually to hop out to safety. His persistent churning had turned the liquid cream into butter!

Draw a picture or a cartoon strip illustrating the story.

Your bumpy road to success

There are critical moments on the way to success; however, if we manage to overcome the temptation to give up the first time, we will be much stronger the second time round and will have a better idea of what to do.

The point marked by arrow 4 on the picture of the 'road to success' is the critical moment when many of us give up; this is exactly the moment we need to anticipate. When we reach this point, we have a choice: we may look for excuses to drop the project, or we may:

- take a rest, rethink our strategy and maybe make some changes

- find someone to support us through the difficult moments

- give ourselves a shake, a good push, and get on with the job!

- Give each student a copy of the picture and tell them that it shows the way we learn anything new.

- Ask students to guess what the stages shown in the picture mean. It is not a simple question so you will probably need to prompt:

  1 fairly fast progress – things seem relatively easy and pleasant

  2 the first 'hiccup'

  3 no sense of progress – we seem to be on a plateau

  4 a sense of total disappointment – low achievement, low energy, no willingness to continue

  5 recovery.

Your bumpy road to success

The picture shows different stages of learning.
Explain what you think the stages marked by the arrows are.

1 ....

2 ....

3 ....

4 ....

5 ....

Response to setbacks

How do you tend to respond to setbacks?
How would you like to respond?

Sometimes dropping a project may be the
right thing to do. However, avoid giving up
on the spur of the moment. When you have
expressed your anger and wallowed in your
disappointment, take time to think. Only when
you have cooled down will you be ready to
make a decision.

> **!** **Asking questions about 'people
> in general' takes the pressure off
> those engaged in the activity and
> makes it easier for them to think
> freely without getting defensive.**

- Ask students to think how people might
  respond to failure and write their thoughts on
  the board.

- Discuss with the group the potential
  consequences of various responses.

- Ask students to think what steps they would
  like to take next time they experience failure
  and are tempted to drop a project (learning a
  language, playing a musical instrument, line
  dancing).

Response to setbacks

How do you respond to setbacks?

Tick your most frequent responses. Your answers may change depending on the kind of setback and on the way you feel, so concentrate on projects that are important to you.

When things go wrong I...

Never	Sometimes	Usually	
☐	☐	☐	decide that life is tough and that 'nothing can ever work for me'.
☐	☐	☐	do it again (and if necessary, yet again!) until I succeed.
☐	☐	☐	take a break and possibly come back to the task later.
☐	☐	☐	feel sorry for myself and find someone to comfort me.
☐	☐	☐	drop the task and decide to do something else.
☐	☐	☐	get very angry, maybe smash things or cry.
☐	☐	☐	blame other people (teachers, parents) or situations for my failure.
☐	☐	☐	....
☐	☐	☐	....

Bumps, hurdles and potholes

There are different kinds of obstacles that prevent us from succeeding.

Some obstacles are external, such as poor health, a dysfunctional family or poor living conditions. Others are of an emotional nature, for example a fear of failure, lack of self-confidence or extreme shyness. Still others are the result of our way of thinking, such as a pessimistic outlook or focusing attention on what goes wrong.

- Hand out the worksheet.

- Ask students to work in pairs and put the obstacles listed where they think they belong on the drawing, writing the numbers:

  – in the head (thoughts)

  – in the heart (feelings)

  – around the body (life situations).

NB Some obstacles may belong in more than one place.

- Ask whether they think that one category of obstacles is more challenging than the others.

- Ask students to identify the toughest hurdle that could prevent them from succeeding.

Bumps, hurdles and potholes

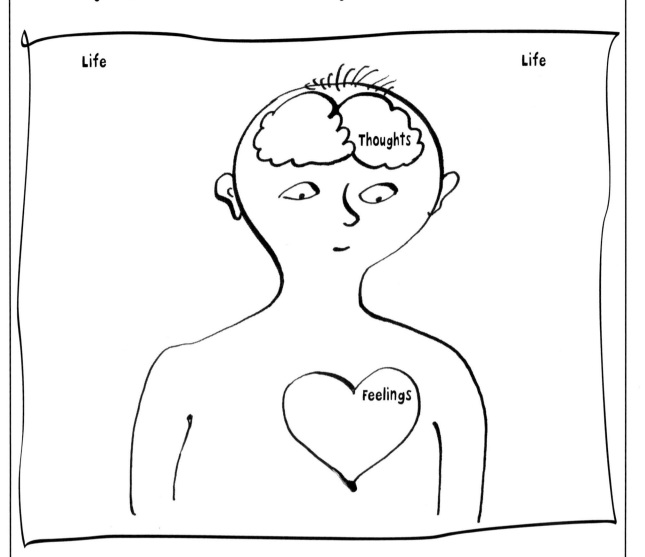

Life   Life

Thoughts

Feelings

1 I am afraid I may fail.

2 I have nobody to support me (emotionally? financially?).

3 I am a victim of life circumstances.

4 I have no role model to follow.

5 I have an inherited illness.

6 I don't know where to turn for help.

7 My family could become homeless any time now.

8 I am rubbish at just about everything.

9 Nobody in my family has any ambition to succeed.

10 I feel very lonely.

11 I blame other people for what happens to me.

12 I think that nobody cares about me.

13 My family is extremely poor.

14 My peers are a bad influence on me.

15 I easily get very angry and become violent.

16 I don't feel motivated to do any work.

17 Some people bully me at school.

18 I have no confidence.

19 People in my family drink, do drugs and fight all the time.

20 I am painfully shy.

Challenges and solutions

When we spend all the time thinking about what it is we don't want, we lose sight of what it is we do want. We lose sight of our goals.

The first thing is to be very clear in our minds why these goals are important to us. The next is to anticipate obstacles that might occur and find ways to overcome them.

Some problems may require more than one attempt to find effective ways of dealing with them. The more possibilities we are aware of, the more likely we will be able to find a solution.

- Photocopy one sheet per two students and cut it so that each challenge and each solution is on a separate strip.

- Ask students to work in pairs and match each listed challenge with potential solutions.

- Ask whether they can think of other ways to deal with the challenges and encourage them to write their thoughts in their journal.

Challenges and solutions

!!!	Extremely difficult family situation	!!!	Complete lack of self-belief
!!!	Sleeping problems	!!!	Serious money problems
!!!	Possible eviction from home	!!!	A short temper and violent outbursts
!!!	Lack of self-discipline	!!!	Paralysing fear of failure
!!!	Giving up easily	!!!	Being bullied

☺	Talk to your tutor or any teacher you feel you can trust	☺	Talk to a friend
☺	Talk to your doctor	☺	Get legal advice
☺	Get in touch with Social Services	☺	Go to your local library and ask the librarian for help
☺	Request counselling sessions	☺	Take an anger management course
☺	Take a confidence training course	☺	Find information on the internet

Notice the positive

Is it possible to become an optimist if your tendency is to focus on the 'empty half of a glass', the 'dark cloud', and only the difficulties ahead? Is it possible to smile more often and frown less? Is it possible to learn to see both the cloud *and* the silver lining, the glass half empty *and* half full, difficulties *and* possibilities?

The fact is that you never know what the future may bring. However, if you have an optimistic outlook and expect positive results:

- You will experience a high level of emotional and physical energy.

- You will have a better chance of enjoying what you're doing.

- You are more likely to persist in striving towards your goal.

- Having spoken to students about some benefits of becoming more optimistic, suggest:

  'So how about having a go at becoming more optimistic, just for the fun of it?'

- Ask students what they are negative about and if they have any ideas about how they could practise becoming more optimistic.

- Tell them to think of a person they often criticise and write two or three positive things about them.

Notice the positive

Think of a person who irritates you.
Draw their face or write their name in the frame.

```
┌─────────────────────────┐
│                         │
│                         │
│                         │
│                         │
│                         │
│                         │
│                         │
│                         │
│                         │
│                         │
└─────────────────────────┘
```

Now imagine you are in a very good mood...
Take a deep breath and write two things you could appreciate in this person.

What I appreciate in .... is:

....

....

Here is a challenge for you:

Every time someone irritates you, make an effort to think of something that is good about them.

People in your life

Some of us have people in our lives who are ready to support us, encourage us and applaud our achievements.

It can be a parent, a grandparent, a friend, a caring teacher, anyone who is inspiring, supportive and truly caring.

- Ask students to think about people in their lives who support, encourage and applaud them.

- Suggest that your students themselves consider becoming supportive and encouraging for somebody they care about.

Identify students who do not have a supportive family, who feel isolated, lonely and not valued.

These are the students who need you the most. Just one person who genuinely believes and encourages a student can make all the difference to their life.

Be this person or find someone who will take on this role.

It is one of the most beautiful compensations of life that no man can sincerely try to help another without helping himself.

Ralph W. Emerson

People in your life

On the thick lines write the names of people who support, encourage and applaud you. On the thin lines write how they do it. Add lines if necessary.

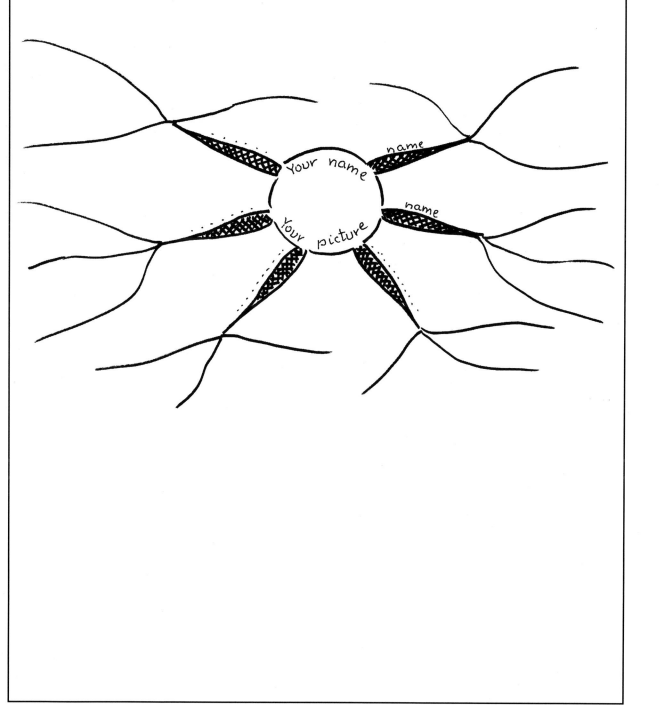

The steps towards success

Every project you undertake in life will go through a number of stages. It is useful to be aware of what they may be.

Imagine you would like to learn something new:

– You make a decision to do it.

– You start doing it.

– You continue doing it.

– You continue doing it!

– You continue doing it!

– You achieve your goal.

– You celebrate your success.

Do the activity yourself and see what your response to challenges is before you give out sheets to your students.

Think about something you tried to do in the past. Which stage did you reach?

0 I kept wishing but did not decide to actually do it.

1 I decided to do it but somehow did not get started … I was just waiting for the right moment …

2 I made a start! However, after a while …

3 I continued doing it for a while. Yet, after some time I …

4 I continued for quite a while but was getting tired / bored / discouraged …

5 I continued for quite some time but seemed to be making no progress, got completely disheartened and dropped the goal.
   OR
   I gave myself a good shake, somehow managed to inject some new enthusiasm and energy into the project and went on …

6 I completed my goal.

7 I celebrated my achievement!

• Show students the picture overleaf and do the activity with them – encourage them to think of real-life situations.

• Tell them that even if they have not succeeded in achieving goals so far, they can decide to change the pattern; the choice is theirs!

The steps towards success

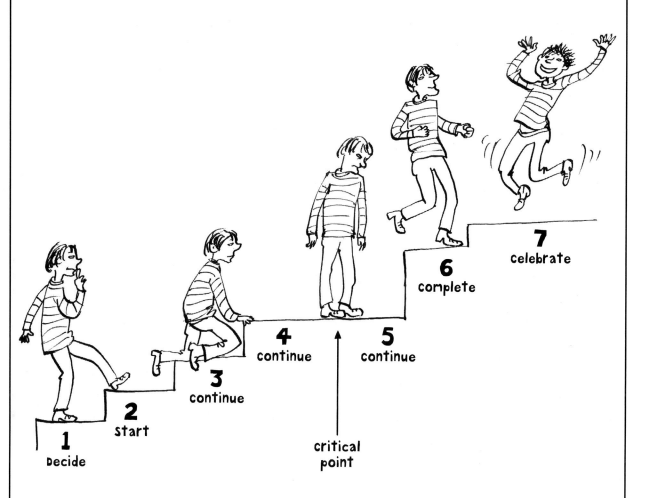

Here are some of the things people do when the critical moment arrives. They:

– ignore the way they feel and push themselves to go forward

– take a break to think things through

– find someone willing to support them

– get new strength by reminding themselves about their goal

– drop the project and look for something else to do

– start again in a different way.

Which do you do most often?
Is it helpful to go on doing that?

Teacher's page

Now or later? Now or never?

We all know people of action; these are the people who make a decision to do something and then simply get on with the job.

Those of us who have a tendency to procrastinate find this readiness for action impressive and a little … irritating. We take a long time to decide and when we have finally made a decision we frequently find reasons to put off the action.

When the mind and body are in the state of inertia, there is a need for some force to shift them out of this state and provoke movement. Ideally, the force comes from within, but what if it doesn't?

The habit of procrastination makes action a real challenge. Overcoming a strong resistance to transform thought into action frequently requires great effort. Many teenagers show tremendous resistance to taking action, especially when pushed to do so. The resistance is powerful and more often than not wins the battle.

- Ask students to think when taking immediate action is essential.

- Ask them to give examples of situations when procrastination can result in a tragedy.

- Ask them to think of times when procrastination may be a saving grace.

- Share with them (if appropriate) your own tendency to put off doing certain things and how this makes you feel.

- Tell them that developing the habit of overcoming the desire to put things off could make their lives infinitely easier.

Now or later? Now or never?

There's no time like now

Write three things you do the very moment you decide:

1 ....

2 ....

3 ....

Now write three things you always put off doing:

1 ....

2 ....

3 ....

21-day practice
Choose one important thing you tend to put off doing and write it in the box.

When you decide to give up putting things off, for 21 days JUST DO IT the moment you realise it needs to be done. Mark your success on the grid; write the date and make a tick whenever you succeed.

1	2	3	4	5	6	7
8	9	10	11	12	13	14
15	16	17	18	19	20	21

Inner drive

What is resilience?
In the context of this chapter, it means determination and perseverance in completing a task in the face of challenges.

What is self-motivation?
It is a push we give to ourselves instead of waiting for someone else to give it to us. It means being driven by our passion, a sense of responsibility or by the prospect of gain.

- Ask students if they know any proverb or saying about perseverance.

- Encourage them to make up a saying of their own.

- Give each student one quote. Tell them to think what it means to them and share their thoughts with others.

- Ask students to read other people's quotes and find one that inspires them. Tell them to write it in their journal.

The apparent ease with which brilliant people perform is often misleading. We cannot even begin to appreciate the amount of preparation that precedes a brilliant performance and makes it appear effortless.

Inner drive

Find the quote you like best, cut it out and glue it in your journal.

Everything you achieve is 10 per cent inspiration and 90 per cent perspiration.	Never, never, never, never give up. *Winston Churchill*
Every failure is an opportunity to begin again more intelligently.	Failure is simply feedback telling you what works and what doesn't.
Mistakes are a necessary part of learning.	It is totally unrealistic and potentially harmful to expect a perfectly smooth road to success.
Focus on your goal, think positively and learn from your mistakes.	Anticipate setbacks and prepare for handling them well. What is wrong with taking an umbrella in case it rains?

Get out of your comfort zone

Are you locked in your comfort zone or do you feel free to move on? Most of us have experienced the fear of change. We feel comfortable in our small world and even the idea of taking steps forward can make us break into a sweat and shake with fear. Everybody experiences fears; there would be no need for courage if people didn't feel scared.

The only way to overcome fear is to do the thing that makes us scared.

Once again we have a choice:

– We can choose to stay in our comfort zone, we can choose not to grow as people, not to learn new things, not to have new experiences, not to take risks.

– We can push ourselves, experience the pain of fear, liberate ourselves from the cage which seems to keep us safe, and experience an exhilarating sense of joy, freedom and achievement.

What will be the consequences of staying put within our limiting world?

What will be the consequences of breaking the cage of fear and spreading our wings?

- Show students the picture and ask them to interpret it.

- Ask students to write all around the cage the names of their 'fear monsters'.

- Ask them to list the advantages of staying within the cage (comfort zone) and the advantages of breaking out of it.

- Remind them that sometimes it may be useful to stay in the cage and at other times it may serve them better to break out of it.

Get out of your comfort zone

What are the fears keeping you in your cage?

The only way to overcome fear is to do the thing that makes us scared.

Role models

Who can be a role model?

– a person we admire

– a person whose characteristics we would like to have

– a person in whose footsteps we would like to follow.

It could be a family member, a family friend, someone we know well, somebody we know about from television or magazines.

It may, however, be a good idea to find out more about our role models so that we know that what we admire in them is not merely some media gimmick!

- Ask students to remember role models from their childhood.

- Tell them to compare their childhood role models with ones they have now.

- Talk with students about the way children idealise their parents only to discover later in life that parents are human!

- If appropriate, talk about your own role models.

- Discuss the suitability of some people to be role models.

- Hand out the worksheet and ask students to write about the person who is their role model now. They can draw them or glue their photograph on to the worksheet.

Role models

....

is my role model.

I admire her / him because

....

....

....

....

....

....

Find a mentor

Who can be a mentor?

A person who:

– cares about you

– accepts you for who you are

– has your interests at heart

– respects you and your ultimate decisions

– you can absolutely trust

– you consider to be wise

– has achieved what you want to achieve

– will find time for you

– listens to your concerns and helps you find your own answers.

A mentor is someone you know personally; they may be a family member, a family friend, a teacher, your friend's parent, a special person in your life.

A mentor is typically someone older than you, with more experience of life. A mentor is invaluable, particularly in moments of crisis, time of doubt and low energy.

- Ask students to think whether they can detect any difference between a role model and a mentor: can a mentor be a role model, can a role model be a mentor?

  – You need to have personal contact with your mentor, whereas you may never meet your role model.

- Get students' ideas as to what kind of person can be their mentor. They can draw them or put their photograph on the worksheet and describe how their mentor supports them.

Find a mentor

This is my mentor.

This is how my mentor supports me:

This is the person who could become my mentor.

I would like my mentor to...

If you don't have a mentor and if you can't think of a person who could become one, keep looking. You will eventually find the right person.

Your ups and downs

Everybody knows that handling failure is tough and frequently a serious challenge. Dealing with anger, blame, frustration and tears takes time and energy, a great deal of thinking and rethinking.

However, success, despite what many people may think, is often not easy to deal with either! It may mean a dramatic change in a life style which can result in confusion, problems with health (stress) and loss of emotional balance, as well as developing unhealthy, even destructive, habits.

- Photocopy the sheet and cut it along the lines.

- Let students pick random quotations and think what they mean.

- Encourage students to share their quotation with four or five partners (one at a time) and listen to what the others have to say.

- Ask everybody to choose their favourite quotation and make a poster to go with the text.

Your ups and downs

✂

Life is like a roller coaster, full of ups and downs; how you handle the ups and the downs will determine your success in life.	You have to build up your 'resilience muscle' if you want to succeed in just about anything.
Leaving your comfort zone and doing what feels uncomfortable is the only way to grow.	There is no person on this planet who does not make mistakes; why should you be the exception?
Take risks when wanting to achieve something. Your decisions may be wrong, they may be right. You will never know, unless you try!	Living within your comfort zone is mere survival. To really live you need to put yourself on the edge of your comfort zone.
Failure is mostly in your mind (you fail when you think you have failed), not necessarily in the outcome of your actions.	We don't always succeed in what we do, but the real failure would be to give up.

Stuck in a rut

A habit is a neuro-physiological programme in our nervous system. On average it takes 21–30 days to create a new neural pattern in our brain. However, if we have been doing something for a very long time, getting rid of an old habit and creating a new one may take longer.

Some thinking habits make a mess of our lives. Every time we think such thoughts as

– I lack confidence

– I can't organise my life

– I am bad at meeting people

– I always forget …

– nobody likes me

… we keep creating stronger and stronger neural patterns in our brain. The stronger the pattern, the more firmly we believe that what we're thinking is true.

- Read the text to students.

- Ask them to think of other examples representing getting 'stuck in a rut'.

- Ask them to draw a poster illustrating the point.

Stuck in a rut

When you drive a car across a muddy field, you leave behind you two tyre tracks.

The second time you drive along the same tracks, they get deeper.

Driving along the third time you find it very difficult to get out of the rut.

Your wheels are almost buried in the mud.

The fourth time – guess what?

YOU GET STUCK!

Don't get stuck in a rut!

Letting go of the need to control

A lot of our anger, our resentment and general dissatisfaction results from the fact that we would like to control things we cannot possibly control.

Wanting to control things we cannot control is the cause of a lot of negativity in our life. It makes us permanently angry and is nothing but a terrible waste of energy.

We need to accept that some things may be controlled only sometimes, under some circumstances, by some people.

- Tell students that while we can control some things in our lives, others are beyond our control.

- Ask them to think of things they can / cannot control and write them on the board.

- If students have not been forthcoming with ideas, give them the worksheets and a list to choose from.

- Instruct them to write in the outer square what they cannot control and in the inner square what it is they *can* control.

- Discuss the importance of knowing the difference.

God grant me the serenity to accept the things I cannot change; courage to change the things I can; and wisdom to know the difference.

Reinhold Niebuhr, 1943

Letting go of the need to control

Let go of what you cannot change and focus on what you can.

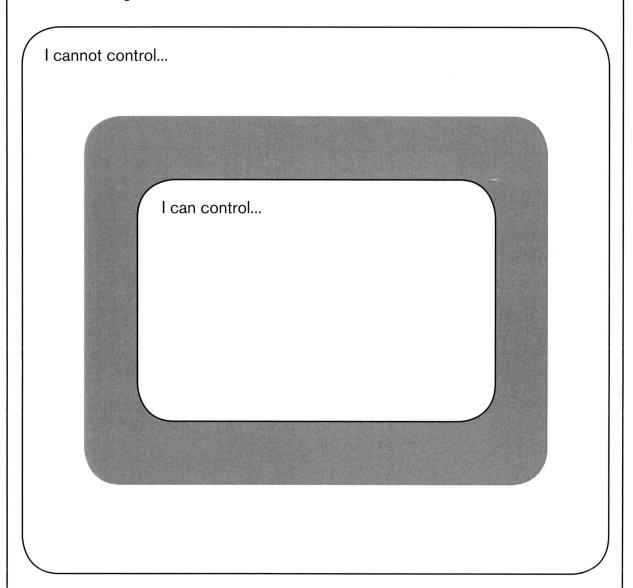

I cannot control...

I can control...

Put the following where they belong:

The weather

My mood

Other people's thoughts

The way I act

The colour of my skin

Where I live

How I talk to people

How people treat me

What I eat

What friends I have

Climbing the walls

We are often warned against 'putting all our eggs in one basket'. It may happen that we put a great deal of effort into trying to achieve a goal only to discover later that this was not the goal we really wanted.

What often follows is loss of heart, frustration, anger with ourselves for all the wasted time, effort and possibly money. Not surprisingly, we feel like giving up altogether.

How can someone get over such a disappointment?

• Tell students:

Imagine that you are standing in the middle of a square surrounded by walls. You are told that on the other side of each wall there is something attractive: an exotic garden, a lake with swans and ducks, a fairground, a forest. Your goal is to get to the lake.

All the walls are high and difficult to climb but each is different.

You are not sure where to put your ladder but finally decide to start climbing up the white stone wall. However, you are not sure you are climbing up the right wall …

• Ask them what they might do if it turns out to be the wrong wall.

• Ask them to think of all the possible options.

Do not judge students' negative response to failure. Just make sure that they are aware of other options; they need to know that after the initial anger they can choose to stop wallowing in misery and begin to look to the future.

Climbing the walls

Cross out the two most *ludicrous* options,
circle two *really dumb* options,
tick the two most *sensible* ones.

If I find out I have been climbing up the wrong wall, I may...

give up

throw a real temper tantrum

cry and scream

lock myself in my room and sleep for a week

try to destroy the wall with my head

swear never to climb any wall again

begin to think what can be done

look more carefully at the walls to see how they differ

decide to give up climbing walls and take up climbing mountains

find ways to make climbing easier and faster

see what other people are doing.

Tips for strengthening resilience

Resilience is:

– **staying power**

– **the ability to motivate yourself when your energy is running out**

– **the ability to persist in the face of frustration**

– **the attitude: 'no matter what, I'll achieve what I have set out to achieve'**

– **the ability to control impulses which may take you away from the goal**

– **the ability to wait for something worth waiting for rather than going for immediate pleasure.**

- Hand out photocopied worksheets and encourage students to think of their own examples.

- Give prompts if students are not forthcoming or when they run out of ideas (see prompts below).

- Ask students to select *one* thing they might consider changing in their lives.

- Encourage them to write about it in their journal.

Prompts

Go easy on your willpower
and avoid situations and people who may distract you from your goal.

– Don't turn the TV on until you have finished your work.

– Take a limited amount of money when you go shopping so you don't overspend.

– Socialise with people who share your values.

Form helpful habits
Good ones can make you, bad ones can break you.

– Do all your work before you go out or turn on your computer.

– Walk / exercise before school (paper round?).

– Take a shower every morning.

Share your resolutions
with someone who will support you.

– Tell your friends about your plans.

– Ask someone to hold you accountable for what you have decided to do.

Keep reminding yourself about your goal

– Display your picture goals where you can see them every day,
  eg in your bedroom, on your computer desktop.

Tips for strengthening resilience

When you decide to build up your staying power, here are some tips for you.
In the spaces provided write what EXACTLY you might do.

Share your resolutions

Go easy on your willpower

Remind yourself about your goals

Form helpful habits

Develop good habits

On average it takes 21–30 days to develop a new habit and two or three times longer to get rid of a well-established yet unwanted habit.

Warning: every time we slip and forget what we have set out to do, we will need to start counting days from the beginning!

Habits make life much easier. When we develop a habit, there is no more need to struggle, exercise our willpower or push ourselves; we do what we need to do without having to think about it.

- Encourage students to think what would be a useful habit they could develop.

- Tell them to formulate it while:
  - making it personal
  - putting it in the present (as if it is already happening)
  - ensuring it is positive (what they want, not what they don't want).

  For example: Every day I put all my dirty clothes in a washing basket.

- Encourage students to make a picture in the oval overleaf representing their new habits.

Develop good habits

My new habit

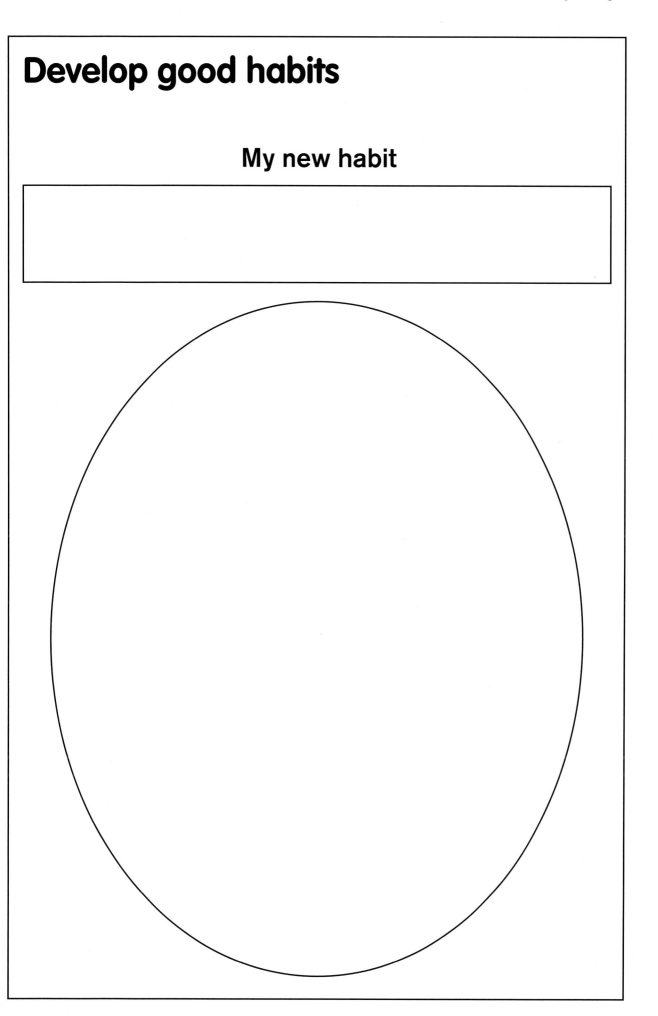